THE ART OF GRANDPARENTING

Loving, Spoiling, Teaching and Playing with Your Grandkids

Witty, Wise and Wonder-filled Stories for New Grandparents

Edited by
Valerie Connelly

Nightengale Press
A Nightengale Media LLC Company
©2009 All Rights Reserved

The ART of Granparenting

Copyright ©2009 Edited by Valerie Connelly
Cover Design ©2009 by Nightengale Press

All rights reserved. Printed in the United States of America. No part of this book may be reproduced or transmitted in any form or by any means, electronic or mechanical, including photocopying, recording, or by any information storage and retrieval system without written permission from the publisher, except for the inclusion of brief quotations in articles and reviews.

If you purchased this book without a cover, you should be aware that this book is stolen property. It was reported as "unsold and de-stroyed" to the publisher, and neither the author nor the publisher has received any payment for this "stripped book."

For information about Nightengale Press please
visit our website at www.nightengalepress.com
Email: publisher@nightengalepress.com
or send a letter to:
Nightengale Press
10936 N. Port Washington Road #206
Mequon, WI 53092

Library of Congress Cataloging-in-Publication Data
Connelly, Valerie, 1947 –
The ART of Grandparenting / Valerie Connelly, Editor
ISBN: 978-1933449-79-1
Non-Fiction, Family Relationships

First Published by Nightengale Press in the USA

10 9 8 7 6 5 4 3 2 1

Printed in the USA at
Lightning Source, Inc.
LaVergne, TN

Contents

Dedication	7
Acknowledgements	7
Introduction	8
Open Letter to New Grandparents Rose Padrick	15
Scary Grandma Stories Carole Blake	25
Becoming a Grandparent without even Trying Carol Muller-Funk	33
Worn Out Nostalgia Bob Kascht	44
Grandparents — Tell Your Story Irene Watson	51
Knocked Sideways by Love Barbara Abercrombie	63
Stories I'd Rather Not Tell Hannah Yakin	70
Surprises, Traditions and the Teacher in Us All Judith Mammay	80
To Grandparents-In-Waiting Rochelle Jewel Shapiro	91
Instant Grandma Gerri Helms	100
How to Become a Go-To Grandma Donne Davis	110
Taking the DISTANCE out of Long-Distance Grandparenting Arlene S. Uslander	122

Grandma's Kaleidoscope
Mary Pansini La Haye ... 130

Not What I Expected
Sharon Bray ... 136

Grandchildren: Your Reward for Raising Your Own
Tim Stewart ... 148

Life Lessons
Chuck McCann ... 154

A Balancing Act of Love
Victoria Zackheim ... 160

The Dirt Floor Visit
Hal Alpiar ... 168

I Like Grandpa
Gene Matthews ... 177

Epilogue
Valerie Connelly ... 184

ABOUT THE AUTHORS ... 192

ROSE PADRICK ... 193

CAROLE BLAKE ... 194

CAROL MULLER-FUNK ... 195

BOB KASCHT ... 196

IRENE WATSON ... 197

BARBARA ABERCROMBIE ... 198

HANNAH YAKIN ... 199

JUDITH MAMMAY ... 200

ROCHELLE JEWEL SHAPIRO ... 201

GERRI HELM ... 202

DONNE DAVIS ... 203

ARLENE USLANDER ... 204

TIM STEWART	205
CHUCK McCANN	206
SHARON BRAY	207
MARY PANSINI LA HAYE	208
VICTORIA ZACKHEIM	209
HAL ALPIAR	210
GENE MATTEWS	211
VALERIE CONNELLY	212
REVIEWS AND GOOD NEWS	213
RESOURCES	219
GREAT BOOKS FOR KIDS AND TEENS	221

Dedication

To new grandparents everywhere who find themselves awed and somewhat baffled by their newly acquired stature in their families, their lives and in their hearts—that of grandparent.

Acknowledgements

Many thanks to all the authors who joined this project with vigorous enthusiasm and who willingly brought to it their wisdom, wit and talents as writers. Their heart-felt honesty shines in every word. Their warmth and desire to share their experiences with those of us who are new to the role of grandparent brings us comfort and optimism.

Introduction

WHEN I FIRST HEARD I was going to be a grandmother, I cried with joy—and then I panicked!

"Why?" you might ask.

Well, primarily because I suddenly realized I had no direct knowledge about how to be a grandmother. I certainly know how to be a mother. Life experience, gained through first-hand, on-the-job-training, with all the fits and starts being a parent requires, eventually taught me what to do. I had a happy childhood filled with not only my own mother and father's loving efforts to bring me up right, but with the eyes, hands and hearts of the mothers and fathers of my childhood friends guiding us all along. I certainly grew up with the comforting knowledge that I would manage to do the best I could with the circumstances of my life as the mother of two daughters. We all do that. But I realized that I was deficient in experience with grandmothers and grandfathers.

"Why?" you might ask, again. If you have a moment, I'll explain.

I was born late in my parents' lives, and they both were the youngest of six with seventeen or more years between their eldest siblings and themselves. My parents were born in 1906 and 1907 and were already in their forties when I surprised them in 1947 by arriving on the first wave of the Baby Boom. Both sets of my grandparents had been born in the mid-1800s. As a result, my grandfathers were long gone before I came along, and my grandmothers were so old—in their eighties—when I arrived on the scene, that they were just waiting to follow their husbands into that Great Beyond.

I do recall meeting my father's mother, Mary Cranston Green, but only three times: once when I was four or five years old, because she gave me a doll, which I kept for thirty years and gave to my first daughter when she was four or five years old; once at her 90th birthday when I was about six; and once for the last time, when she was ninety-eight and I was fourteen. By that time she was confined to a bed. We had traveled to visit her in the rest home so my father could see her before she died. When it was my turn to greet her, I was told to sit on the edge of her bed. I looked at her and smiled, not sure what to do or say.

"You look European," she said.

I recall saying something informative like, "Well, my mother is Swedish, maybe that's why."

But that's all I can remember of her, except for her sparkling blue eyes, her beautiful, flowing white hair, and the long, isolated, singleton whiskers poking out from odd places on her cheeks, chin, and upper lip as she smiled at me. She passed away shortly thereafter, and hers was the first funeral I ever attended. I watched her one and only picture fade away with time, and I read the family collection of her stories and poems twenty years after she had died, only then to learn she was deeply religious, she loved flowers, and she was mildly clairvoyant. All in all, I never really had a grandmother or grandfather of my own. I had no first-hand knowledge of a grandmother's hug or a grandfather's tall tale.

By the time I began to have my own children in my late twenties, my retired, golf-and-bridge-playing parents lived in distant, sunny California. I lived with my emerging family where I had grown up, in windy, snowy, blustery Chicago. Back then, in the mid-1970s and early 1980s, the cost of air travel was well beyond my means. My parents were getting on in years, and flying was not easy for them. So, they ended up being essentially unavailable as grandparents for my two daughters. I can actually count on only one hand the number of times my parents saw my children from birth to teenage years.

My in-laws lived closer, just a six-hour drive away. We arranged short, week-end visits two or three times a year, but always with us parents in the vicinity and never with grandchildren only. We did travel with them for two weeks to Europe once, with my older daughter who was about four years old at the time. They were good and loving grandparents, but I really missed out on learning how to grandparent from them. Many of my friends, whose parents lived closer by and who could spend more day-to-day time engaged in the lives of their grandchildren, learned first-hand what worked and what didn't. They saw how their parents did what they needed to do as grandparents. My friends learned the tricks of the trade, both from having grandparents of their own, and also from learning how their parents behaved with their own children.

As I contemplate acquiring that honorable new name—Grammie, or Granny, or Nana, or Grandma, or Mimi, or whatever it will eventually be—I realize that I have a lot to learn. I hunger for that wisdom I wish I had gained by familial osmosis from my elders. I can imagine what kind of grandmother I want to be, but I'm not sure I know how to do it. Like so many others who missed out on grandparent education in early childhood, I see myself going to the grandparenting well only to find it dry. No lasting, clear model of grandparent behavior flows forth from my past. I have said many times over that I know what I wish might have transpired. I think I know what grandparenting lessons I missed in my childhood and during my time as a young mother. But it is hard to conjure up any meaningful guidance from lessons you know you didn't learn.

Children don't come with instruction books. Neither do grandchildren. I don't know about the rest of you, but I am certain I'm going to need *HELP* to be a good grandparent. I expect that there are lots of others who need help too. Where will we find the insights, the wisdom, even the patience others gain from observation and acceptance? How will we invent the grandparent wheel yet again without even a shadow of a blue print? Perhaps the answers will come mostly through the doing of it.

But, I sure do want to read up on the subject—just as reading up on pregnancy helped me to know what would and could happen—just as reading up on several different theories and practices of child-rearing helped to sort out what parenting philosophy might fit me as a new mother and what wouldn't. And to recognize how behaviors learned through familial osmosis are ever-present in our social DNA, I'll bet, like me, you can remember many times you've heard your mother or father's words flowing from your own mouth when presented with behavior from your children you wished to modify one way or another. Soaking up the examples of our elders serves us, for better or for worse, in the journey from childhood to the grave. So does curiosity. So does trying to learn from others.

The many questions I have about how to be a grandparent inspired this book. To achieve a modicum of *savoir faire*, I decided to reach out to the writing community I am privileged to know to find authors who could express their grandparenting experiences with humor, information and insight for me and all the others who might feel unsettled by their own lack of quality time with grandparents. In part, it will address the long-distance separations and time-deprived lives endured by modern American families, who are scattered across the land and whose children don't even know their relatives, much less see them regularly. These pages should also bring a few tears and plenty of laughter as you read the various ways in which these authors met the challenges in their own lives as grandparents.

There is honesty here. You will know something more of what to expect when that first bundle of joy—and personality, mischief and braggadocio—comes into your life, and then the next one, and the next. Some of our authors are already Masters of the Art of Grandparenting, with as many as twenty-three grandchildren and a smattering of great-grandchildren. Some are newly initiated by having just joined the club. Others had grandchildren of their own, and then gained a new brood through re-marriage later in life. There could be as many glimpses into the world of grandparents and grandchildren as there are grandparents and grandchildren, and as such it would be impossible to chronicle them all. So, it is my hope that the letters in this book will open a door wide enough to give us a peek into life as a grandparent, while offering a broad enough spectrum of viewpoint and richness of experience to help us begin this new journey with some helpful perspective.

This collection of letters is a gift to all present and future newbie grandparents, who need tips, tricks and real-life guidance as they first take on the role of grandparent. I hope you enjoy reading it as much as I have enjoyed bringing it to life.

By the way, I have a hunch that to be a good grandparent you just have to jump into the vat with two feet and mash the grapes, or leap into the water and swim the rapids, or in your own way just do whatever it takes to be part of your grandchild's life. I suspect that making every moment count, that *being there* will be the true key to mastering the art of grandparenting.

Valerie Connelly
Publisher, Nightengale Press

The Art of Grandparenting

Open Letter to New Grandparents

Rose Padrick

WELCOME—WELCOME—WELCOME! to the most wonderful club in the universe!

Whether you're Grammy, Poppi, Nana, Gigi or have chosen your very own special name, with just the simple act of entering your world, this new addition or additions have forever changed your very soul. I thank The One Above every day for blessing me with sixteen amazing second generation additions to my soul. I still can't believe how incredibly lucky my husband and I are.

Grandchildren are indeed your second chance to enjoy the perfection of each rose—this time without the thorns.

If you are of my vintage, it may take a little while to figure out that caring for babies has changed drastically in the years since our equipment has been discontinued.

We were *with child*. Modern ladies are *pregnant*.

We wore blouses gathered under our breasts and flared out like a circus tent lest anyone see our bulging belly, even in silhouette. Modern ladies wear stretch shirts that accentuate the beach ball sitting in their laps.

The Art of Grandparenting

We boiled everything: water for formula, glass bottles, nipples, feeding spoons. Modern mothers use bottled water for formula and put everything else in the dishwasher.

We mixed 16 ounces of the boiled water with 13 ounces of canned milk with 2 ounces of clear corn syrup, and poured it into the boiled glass bottles. Modern mothers take the plastic bottles and nipples out of the dishwasher, pour in 6 ounces of bottled water, 2 scoops of powder and Dad feeds the baby.

Diapers were held together with pins and covered with plastic pants. They had to be changed at least hourly during waking hours. They were rinsed and stored in diaper pails in a bleach solution. They were washed in more bleach, rinsed twice to get rid of all that bleach, rinsed again with fabric softener, and hung on the clothes line to dry. Modern diapers come complete with tape or Velcro, only need changing every couple of hours, are twisted in plastic and then thrown away.

Most of the changes are wonderful. Due to better prenatal care, babies are healthier now than ever before, dads are much more involved in the baby, and both parents have more time and energy to just enjoy the baby and each other.

But some things will never change. It still takes thirty-five pounds of stuff to transport a six-pound baby from home to the grocery store. Moms the world over still pace for hours with colicky babies, have a zombie-like appearance and stains on the shoulders of good blouses. Babies smile and coo right up to the moment they are being shown off, at which time they begin a three-hour, non-stop scream fest. But, the most important thing that will never change is a Grandparent's love.

Doctors say, even before birth, babies are able to recognize familiar voices and they begin recognizing faces almost at birth, this gives grandparents a wide spoiling window.

The Art of Grandparenting

It may take a little while, but you will soon learn it's okay to enjoy the time spent holding and rocking a colicky infant to give Mom a little break without feeling guilty, because you will be getting a full night's sleep later on. Staring into the unblinking, seemingly all-knowing eyes of a newborn, while nourishing his body with a warm bottle was even more indescribably wondrous to my grandmother heart than it was when the infant was my own. I usually took this opportunity to regale the child with tales of how much fun we would be having as we go through this life together. This chatter seemed to help the baby connect my voice with my face—and with fun a little later.

Welcoming a new grandchild not of your gene pool is every bit as awesome. We became the proud grandparents of a beautiful ten-year-old, who we began to spoil the moment she shyly ventured into our large boisterous family during a holiday dinner. Since her biological grandmother was very ill at the time and subsequently passed away, I was honored to become a sort-of surrogate. This girl has blossomed into one of the most wonderful college students I have ever had the pleasure of hugging. I believe that hugging is the key to reaching straight to any child's heart.

If you have the good fortune to live close enough to your grandchildren to watch as they grow, please take every opportunity to spend time with them. Unfortunately, most grandparents are employed now-a-days, but the times I was able to take a half-day off work to 'kidnap' a grandchild from daycare and treat him to ice cream have become some of the most memorable hours, for myself, for the child and for the mother—for varied reasons concerning the ice cream before dinner.

Allow me to explain my actions. My husband and I have five children, four of them girls. We survived five teenage passages from child to adult, all running the gamut of wails, tears and broken

The Art of Grandparenting

bones five different times in five different ways. Having done that, I now believe that grandparents have certain responsibilities: that grandchildren are your reward for not throttling your teenagers and that vengeance may not be ours. But, I'll admit there are times when retribution makes my world go around. And, I am having a wonderful time living my beliefs.

Having grandchildren ranging in age from crawling to college affords me many opportunities to put my beliefs into action. As you become more comfortable with the role of grandparent, you will carve your own path in your grandchildren's lives. Allow me to share a few of my better days just to get you started on the right path.

When our children were young we counted every gram of sugar and caffeine that entered their little bodies. I made sure they had as many of the seven food groups as I could put in their mouths, scrape off their chins, put in their mouths, scrape off their chins, et cetera, et cetera, et cetera. I also dealt with a grandparent who gave them sips of her iced tea with sugar at bedtime and ice cream for breakfast. So, I'm just passing on a family tradition, albeit enjoying it more. To keep peace in the family, I have become quite good at covert feeding. A half spoonful of vanilla pudding quickly pushed into an appreciative baby's mouth while Mom's head is turned is easier to get away with than the same amount of blue birthday cake frosting.

The child's age is also a factor. I can share a spoonful of cake, a bit of ice cream, and a few sips of soda with a nine-month-old, but all his mom will see is a "Hi Mom, I love you" smile from both of us. The appearance of innocence reigns.

A six-month-old is still in the tattletale stage. A bit of blue frosting will somehow double in the few seconds it spends inside his mouth, dribble down his chin, slime his little fist, which somehow always finds it's way to Grammy's hair, and drips onto his new shoes, all in the couple of seconds it takes for his mother to glance over and

THE ART OF GRANDPARENTING

catch us. At which time I declare, "I have no idea how the child was able to reach far enough to grab my cake!" and escape by rushing out of the room to clean the child's face.

You may begin to notice more and more similarities between the recently mobile grandchild and yourself. I have found the moment the child discovers that those two things his mother keeps forcing shoes onto have the power to transport him is the last moment he crawls. But, one minor problem is that many times a child takes longer steps on one side than the other, causing those chubby little legs to carry him in wide arcs, and looking just a little surprised about where he ends up—rarely in the place he was aiming for.

I can hardly believe how many times a day I find myself in places where I have absolutely no idea why I am there. It comes as no surprise that, when children find themselves in an unplanned space, they grab the first thing not nailed down and pop it into their mouths. It also comes as no surprise that, when most of my *"Why the heck did I come in here?"* moments end in the kitchen, I pop anything that is not nailed down into my mouth.

I think the most striking similarity between grandmas and grandkids is the way we both react to a big wide smile and a snuggly hug. We both smile bigger and snuggle closer, especially if we are smiling and hugging each other. That is the absolute best place for anyone to end up, no matter where you were aiming for, or how you got there.

I love going to my grandchildren's sports events. The enjoyment is intensified by the fact that, this time around, I was not the one picking them up at school, taking them to practice, taking them home, bathing them, cooking their dinners, and helping with their homework. All I have to do is go to the game, cheer and try not to get in trouble.

The Art of Grandparenting

Recently, when one of my special little guys veered off line to bring me a flower during a soccer game, he was followed closely by an overly excited Shrek look-alike in a coach's shirt. Just as my little guy reached me, the ogre reached him. I saw one massive paw stretch toward a little shoulder and instinct kicked in. I realized my little guy had darted behind me when I heard an awed, "Awwriiiight Grammy!"

I found out how much trouble a Grammy can get into for shin kicking. BUT—I went to the *time-out seat* with my head held high, clutching a slightly bedraggled Black-Eyed Susan, all the while basking in the admiration of a group of two-foot-tall Munchkins in uniform.

Sometimes, we have to be a little inventive in our approach to making memories. A few months ago, I accompanied my daughter and her family to a theme park so I could help keep my grandson *reined in* while Mom and Dad had a few moments to enjoy the park sans "Can we?" and "I want." The weather was beautiful, the park was beautiful, Mom and Dad wandered ahead a few yards. Beautiful!

A contest to see who could hop on one foot the longest while holding hands—I won—led to a contest to see who could hop on one foot the longest without holding hands—he won. I was able to stay on tip-toe longer, but he could walk backwards with his eyes crossed the longest. All of the above were done in spurts, while the adults—Mom and Dad—were otherwise occupied. My daughter will someday forget there's a picture floating around of her bending over the dolphin tank, but I sure hope he and I don't ever forget taking it.

One of the absolute best perks of being a grandparent is the sleepover.

Allowing the wee ones to stay up as later than *anyone else in the whole world,* guarantees late mornings—sometimes. Slipping quietly into the back yard in bare feet to wiggle toes in damp grass and listen to the sounds of the night is magical.

The Art of Grandparenting

Breakfast is also a wonderful privilege. Granting a wish of "Chocolate Everything!" is so gratifying, it's almost worth the explanation to parents later. Chocolate chip pancakes, made with milk and eggs—that's healthy isn't it? Maple syrup and chocolate milk are great sleepover fare.

Spending the morning in deep conversation, "Do you think the blobby thing on the Sponge Bob show is a plankton or a jelly fish?" I ask. "Must be a jelly fish—I've never seen plankton wear blue shorts," he says. One of my more shining moments—I think—came when my grandson exclaimed, "Tommy said he has the bestest Gramma, but I told him MY Grammy is the bestest. You're bigger than his and your face is crinklier than his Gramma's!"

Remember, each child is his own individual, and watching each personality emerge is made more fascinating viewed from a grandparent's perspective.

I admit it's a tad difficult to just watch from the sidelines without trying to coax grandchildren one way or another, but for the most part I quietly cross my fingers and mentally try to steer them in the right direction. I have been rewarded many times over.

Twin granddaughters changed their majors almost monthly while in college, but knowing they each settled on a vocation that will be enriching the lives of others who are in the midst of life-changing emergencies pops the buttons off this old Grammy's shirt.

I have a grandson who is the offspring of wonderfully musically talented parents but showed absolutely no interest in music until his eleventh birthday. Then he took off like a rocket! I unashamedly bawl like a baby every time I watch him coax the voices of angels from his violin. This also triggered his siblings, who are each mastering their own instruments, to join him in the pursuit of musical perfection. I have a feeling I'll be tearing up a lot in the years to come.

I have many other success stories but I think you get the gist.

THE ART OF GRANDPARENTING

Remembering how much I appreciated an evening out once in a while when my children were little, I try to make it a point to offer to babysit whenever needed. As in everything else, I put a personal spin on the evening.

A dear friend of mine recently became an instant grandmother when her son married a wonderful lady with two small children. Eagerly awaiting her first babysitting invitation, she confided she wanted to be very careful to follow the parents' rules and never step over the line to becoming an interfering grandmother. She then asked me—of all people—for tips.

I wrote down a few items in chronological order that I feel are most important, and I'd like to share them with you.

1. Arrive early toting a bag full of nutritious snacks and a few good books.

2. Smile and nod while Mom and Dad drone on and on about emergency numbers, bedtimes, not waking the baby up, and which T.V. shows are absolutely forbidden.

3. Lock the door and watch to be sure Mom and Dad actually make it out of the driveway.

4. Send one of the older kids out to get the bag holding the REAL goodies out of its hiding place under your car seat.

5. Wake the baby, savoring the moment he opens those beautiful green eyes, recognizes you, and his whole face smiles at you.

6. Turn the radio on LOUD and let everybody dance in the kitchen while you make microwave Smores.

7. While the Smores cool, bunny hop into the back yard and howl at the moon.

8. Wolf down the treats (with milk of course) so you can enjoy a game of hide and seek in the (almost) dark.

9. Change the baby's pajamas—and try to rinse all the chocolate out before hiding them in the washer.

The Art of Grandparenting

10. Pop in a video, in an attempt to quiet the sugar-filled and energy-laden children before Mom and Dad come home.

11. Make a quick exit when they do get home, hastily explaining the baby just woke up when you went to check on him and you are sure he will go right back down.

12. Deny everything! Especially when Dad calls the next day wondering how the baby managed to change his own P.J.s and why his neighbor reported hearing really strange noises coming from somewhere in the vicinity of his back yard.

13. Don't sweat the repercussions, the parents will eventually forget you didn't follow their silly rules, but hopefully the kids never will.

I guess what I'm really trying to say is to relax and concentrate on enjoying each grandchild The One Above blesses you with. I live by the adage He gave children parents to make the rules and regulations to help them grow into fine, upstanding adults. He gave children grandparents to bend the rules, disregard the regulations to help them grow into fine adults that had the bestest Grammys in the world. And, He gave us grandchildren because He loves us.

the Art of Grandparenting

Tips & Tricks

Chatter to help the baby connect your voice with your face—and with fun a little later.

Hugging is the key to reaching straight to any child's heart. Engage in big smiles and snuggly hugs.

Carve your own path in your grandchildren's lives.

Become quite good at covert feeding.

Go to your grandchildren's sports events.

Host sleepovers allowing the wee ones to stay up as later than *anyone else in the whole world.*

Breakfast is also a wonderful privilege. Grant the wish for "Chocolate Everything!"

Spend the morning in deep conversation about anything they want to talk about.

Watch from the sidelines without trying to coax grandchildren one way or another.

Offer to babysit whenever needed and put a personal spin on the evening.

Relax and concentrate on enjoying each grandchild.

Scary Grandma Stories

Carole Blake

You wouldn't think being a Grandma was scary; but just wait till it happens to *you!* I have experienced a few very scary moments already, and my grandchildren are only six and two-and-a-half, and there could be more coming at any time! Eek!

First of all, the word "grandmother" is defined in Webster's dictionary as follows: The mother of one's father or mother; also galled *grandam.*" And then *"grandam"* is defined as "*Old Woman, from the French.*" It's the "Old Woman" part that *scared* me the most! *I wasn't thrilled with Mr. Webster at this point!* I remember when I was giving birth to my first child, my daughter, and my mother was quite concerned about what she would be called by her grandchild. "Grandma" made her feel old; she preferred "Nana." My mother-in-law, whose name was Jean, wanted "Jean-Jean." I have a small business in which I write Candle Lighting poems for Sweet 16s, Bar Mitzvahs, and parties, and I've come across the most diverse names of grandmothers: MeeMaw, Bubbie, LayLay, KeeKee, BahBah — just to name a few. *Try rhyming those gems!*

THE ART OF GRANDPARENTING

When I was a young mom, with my daughter and my son, I was cool, calm, and collected. I remember that my son would occasionally wake up in the middle of the night with a horrendous croup cough. It was very disturbing because he was having trouble breathing, but I knew what to do. I would carry him to the bathroom, close the door, and put on the hot shower. Once the room got all steamy and hot, his croup would go away, and he'd be fine. Easy! If this ever happened now, to either of my grandsons, I think I'd have a heart attack!

A few years ago, when my oldest grandchild, Jake, was about three, he had a 'sleepover' at my house. Aside from worrying obsessively and constantly about the possibility of his climbing the fourteen carpeted stairs—*which he was not used to since he lived in a New York City apartment all on one floor*— leading up to our bedrooms, I was fine. The second he went anywhere near the top or bottom step—*poof*—I was in front of him. *This was the best aerobic exercise I'd had in years!* He wasn't too hungry at dinner, but I didn't think much of that. We played puzzle games; we colored; we threw ping pong balls into a basket. We were having fun!

And then, suddenly, something came over Jake, and he seemed quite listless and just not himself. I put my hand on his forehead, and lo and behold, he was *boiling!* How did this happen? And then he was crying; screaming, really. He was fine when he had arrived, but now he definitely had a fever. And I didn't have any Children's Tylenol. My husband was out of town on business, and so I had to maneuver a screaming, flailing Jake into the car seat, and I drove to a nearby Seven/Eleven in search of the Tylenol. I extricated him from the car seat—*they're so tricky now-a-days*—and flew into the store with him in my arms. I immediately found the medication, grabbed it, and then waited in line at the cash register to pay.

My luck, the first person in line was playing the lottery and talking annoyingly on his cell phone to *whomever* about which numbers to pick. "7, 19, 24, 38...or whaddya think about..."

THE ART OF GRANDPARENTING

It was at this moment that I kind of exploded. "I'VE GOT A SICK CHILD HERE! LET ME PAY AND GET OUT— PLEASE!" Well, *I didn't really say "please," but I don't think you could print what I really said.*

When we got home, I gave Jake the medicine, I gently rubbed a cool washcloth over his forehead, I wiped away the drips from his little nose and eyes. He finally fell asleep, and he felt much better in the morning. But *I* didn't sleep for one minute! *That* was scary! *I wonder if that guy ever won the lottery? If so, he owes me big time!*

Towards the end of the next day, after having delivered Jake safe and sound back to his New York apartment, I received a telephone call from my daughter. She told me that she had taken Jake to the pediatrician, and that he was OK, but that he had Pink Eye. *"Pink Eye!"* I murmured worriedly. But according to my daughter, he was treated for it, and it was basically no longer a problem. Maybe not for *them*—but *my* eyes were really starting to bother me! I think Pink Eye is kind of *scary*.

And then, of course, a couple years later, Jake's little brother, Davis, was born. The night of his birth brings to mind an old movie called "Adventures in Babysitting." There I was, at home in the Long Island suburbs, gingerly removing two beautifully cooked Cornish game hens from the oven. To keep the 'movie theme,' imagine sound effects of a phone ringing: *ring, ring!* "Mom! I'm in labor! I need you to come and babysit Jake!" Somewhat surprised since my daughter wasn't due till the following week, I ignored the hens, packed a quick bag and was on my way to Manhattan. My daughter really needed me since her husband was out of town on business. *Hmm...that's beginning to sound like an interesting male trait in my family!*

Next scene: There I am on the Long Island Expressway at night anxiously trying to figure out how, exactly, to get to my daughter's new apartment in Battery Park City. One week before, I had helped

THE ART OF GRANDPARENTING

her move there from midtown—*which is easy to get to*—and I found it very tricky to negotiate those downtown streets—*especially at night*—and especially with my daughter in labor. *Sound effect: SCARY music.*

Now I was lost! I knew I was in the Financial District, but lost—*lost*—LOST! I spotted a police car— *thank goodness*—rolled down my window and pleaded. "Please, sir, help me find West Street. My daughter's having a baby!" The kind officer seemed to understand my dilemma, and he personally led me to my daughter's apartment building. I parked my car in the—*cheap at $45-day*—garage and sped up to her apartment on the 26th floor.

She was there, waiting with Jake and her friend who was going to accompany her by taxi to the hospital, which was uptown. My instructions were very clear: Read Jake a story at bedtime, 9:30; he will wake up at 9:30 AM the next morning, and give him juice, cereal, and milk. Make sure he goes to the bathroom, get him dressed, take him in your car and drive up to the hospital to be with all of us. *Simple, right? Well—not really!*

The going-to-sleep part was easy—for Jake—not for me! I was too keyed-up and excited to sleep, not to mention that I am never an easy sleeper under the best of circumstances—*see scary story of Jake-with-a-fever above*—and so I was prepared to be up for the night—which I was. Also, I was concerned that my son-in-law would be coming back to the apartment, and if I bolted the door on the top, he wouldn't be able to enter. So I didn't bolt the door. *SCARY music again.*

At 8:00 AM, after an entire sleepless night, I suddenly heard a huge noise. SLAM! BANG! What on earth was that? I immediately ran out of bed to check on Jake. I thought he might have fallen out of his bed. I looked in his room: NO JAKE! The kitchen—the bathroom: NO JAKE! Oh—My—God! We're on the 26th floor in

THE ART OF GRANDPARENTING

a Manhattan apartment building, and my three-and-a-half-year-old grandson knows how to operate the elevator! He knows how to press all the buttons! *Especially mine!*

I then ran to the front door and pulled it open, ready to search every floor of the high rise building. *Sound effect of screams—like in "Psycho."* And there, standing calmly in his Spider Man underpants and T-shirt with his hands on his hips, was Jake.

"I was looking for my Mom," he said.

Needless to say, I gritted my teeth, grabbed him by the shoulder, and said—*as sweetly as possible*— "GET IN HERE!" *The SLAM/BANG, by the way, had been the sound of the apartment door slamming—a sound I never want to hear again—ever!*

After breakfast, with hands shaking—*mine*—we drove to the hospital where Mom, Dad, and baby Davis were all doing fine. I sat on the chair next to my daughter's bed, and they placed little Davis in my arms with Jake looking on, and all I could think of was, "Please... no sequels!"

And then there was the time not too long ago that Davis was recovering from surgery and had stitches in his head. *The surgery, thank goodness, was minor and was very successful.* I was sitting with him and his big brother in their playroom, and I watched as Jake picked up a toy golf club and began to swing like Tiger Woods. Don't get me wrong—I'm sure Jake will make the Pro Tour one day, but I was so nervous that he would accidentally hit Davis right in the head—I almost fainted. My daughter, however, calmly inserted herself between the two boys, and the danger was averted. But still— *SCARY!*

But let me say right now that being a grandma isn't always scary. For instance, once in a while you get the opportunity to just sit back and realize how very brilliant your grandchild is. One day last year, when I was visiting my daughter and her family, Jake invited me to accompany him to the bathroom. Not one to reject any invitation from any of my progeny, I said, "Sure."

So, as he was sitting on the 'throne,' doing his 'business,' with great concentration, he asked me, "Grandma, how old are you?"

I replied, "How old do you *think* I am, Jake?"

He thought about it for a while and said, "Well—my Mom is thirty-five." He looked at me and thought for a bit, and then he said, "So—are you thirty-six?"

Bingo! I *told* you—he's brilliant!

And talking about brilliant—I must give equal time to my younger grandson, Davis. He's a two-and-a-half-year-old New York City kid. Certain days I travel into the city to the Financial District to meet him and the babysitter who takes him to a place called the Winter Garden. It's right near the area where the old World Trade buildings stood. It's a lovely, indoor huge open space where babies, kids, teens, and adults, congregate on a daily basis. There are shops, places to eat, and it's sunny and bright. I've been told that Davis has forsaken his fellow toddlers and has instead befriended several senior citizens there. Actually, he thinks his best friend is an eighty-seven-year-old man named Arnie.

They adore him there. He's got such a sweet nature, but, take it from me—he's got a real competitive streak in him. For instance, one day I was playing with him while his older brother was taking a swimming lesson at an indoor pool. We had purchased a small bottle of water in a vending machine. I took the cap off for him, and he grabbed it from me. So now he's holding this blue cap with a mischievous look in his eyes, and he says, "Grandma—hedth a tahth?"

Baffled, I looked at him quizzically, and said, "What, Davis? What are you saying?"

"HEDTH A TAHTH...HEDTH A TAHTH!!" he repeated.

The Art of Grandparenting

And then it hit me! He was saying, "Heads or Tails?" *What did it matter that the blue cap was exactly the same on both sides!*

"Oh—I see! I get it! OK—Heads!"

And so Davis threw the water bottle cap way up in the air. It finally landed, and he quickly picked it up. I asked, "Did I win?"

He looked at it very carefully—and then up at me sadly. "TAHTH...YOU LOOTHE!"

So now, you might wonder, "How does one get over the *scary* part of being a Grandma?" Well, you *could* go right for the Valium, but I don't really recommend that, especially if you're babysitting and need to be on your toes and at your best. You could try Yoga and meditation, but it might be hard to meditate with a screaming hysterical child in the room—or worse—in the car. I have found that the more time I spend with the boys, the more comfortable I've become. And as they're getting older, they listen better. Of course, now that Jake is six and a half and Davis is almost three, they are extremely physical with one another. The old saying "boys will be boys" is certainly true in this case. It involves major pillow fights on the bed, pushing matches on the sidewalks of New York, dancing on tables in pizza parlors, and all kinds of other exciting stuff. All just perfect for their Nervous Nellie Grandma! My daughter, however, is extremely nonchalant about it all, and I know she probably thinks that I get too nervous. However, *I* keep saying to myself, "I can't wait till *she's* a Grandma and sees how scary it is!" *I used to say, "I can't wait till she's a mother!" but now I guess I'll just have to wait a bit longer! A lot longer! I hope I'm still around, because it'll be extremely satisfying to see!*

So all in all, the scariness has seemed to go away.

The Art of Grandparenting

Tips & Tricks

And there are definite things you can do to prevent most of the scary things from happening:

Always keep Children's/Baby Tylenol in the house.

Always bolt the top lock —where the kid can't reach— in a New York City apartment.

Never let toy golf clubs in a room with a grandchild who just had stitches.

Always lie about your age to your grandchildren.

Always bet "tails" (tahth).

If you adhere to all of the above, I guarantee that you won't be scared any more—well, at least not *AS* scared! So now, you can just sit back, relax, and enjoy! Every moment is precious!

Becoming a Grandparent without even Trying

Carol Muller-Funk

THE BRIDE HAD MADE THE LONG WALK down the church aisle. Nervously she had stood in front of the host of family and friends who had come to witness the wedding. The organ played sweetly. The soloists sang. Candles burned softly—and then the magic words at last: "I do!"

Done!

As I look back on that happy day, little did I realize then what those two little words held in store for me. Not only had I just committed to becoming the sixty-five-year-old wife to a sixty-eight-year-old man, but in addition I had just become an instant grandmother of eight more grandchildren in addition to the seven I already had at the time! Fifteen grandchildren—and half of them without even trying! My first question as I looked into the faces of their eager, beautiful, somewhat doubtful expressions I wondered to myself, "Where do we go from here? What are my expectations of these new additions to my family? What are their expectations of me?"

The Art of Grandparenting

It has been seven years into the journey now, and as I reflect back on those years I have mixed feelings. There are things that went okay, and then there are things that I wish I could change if I had to do it all over again. It has been a painful journey at times. It has been a joyful experience at times. My hope was to become a part of this family, sharing my new husband and yet knowing I would always be on the outside looking in.

In the beginning my new mate and I were so elated with the marriage that we really didn't give much thought to the grandchildren, but as time passed I noticed I was seeing less and less of my own grandkids. They had always been such a blessing to me. There was nothing I cherished more than to have them pile around me while I read some book to them, or fixed their favorite dessert, or took them swimming in our backyard pool. I felt, somehow, in remarrying that I had lost something between us. Our family was not the same anymore and I was lonesome for the way it used to be. With a new partner sharing the house, I did not always feel comfortable having the grandkids there like I used to. I sold the house with the swimming pool when I remarried so we could move into our own home. I missed those times together in the backyard pool. It was just so different and I yearned for the past. Instead of having grown to grandmother of fifteen I felt almost like I had become grandmother of no one.

I knew things would be different once my remarriage took place. Just how different I had no way of knowing. I am a believer of "once putting the hand to the plow, never look back," type of person, but sometimes it is hard not to look back. Sometimes the plow does some uneven terracing I have to admit!

The journey actually began when my new husband and I had discussed the possibility of marriage after losing our spouses. (See Golden Love: Nightengale Press: 2005) It seemed a simple

The Art of Grandparenting

enough thing. We had met on an Alaskan tour and after a six-month relationship decided we wanted to tie the knot permanently. We both loved to travel and wasted no time in planning trips to take together. Though we had discussed the bringing together of our two families at that time we were so involved in our personal relationship that it seemed a trivial thing. It would all work out, we were sure.

Knowing my new husband and his recently deceased wife was a close-knit family, just as my dear, deceased husband and I had been with our own grandchildren, I really did not know what my role would be with these newly adopted grandchildren. Nor did my new husband know his role, I am sure. Looking back, no doubt the grandkids were wondering what their role was also.

Now that there has been ample time to reflect the period of growth, I pass on some of those experiences. I understand they will not apply directly to all cases, but I feel in certainty that there will be basic characteristics we can all relate to.

In this day of age, there is the ever-growing potential of becoming an instant grandparent without even trying. As more and more young parents with children make the choice to divorce and remarry, or as in our case lose spouses and choose to remarry in late age, ready-made grandchildren come with the package. How to deal with them opens up a whole new world of concern. Of course, you want above all to be accepted and loved, but how does one go about accomplishing this without guidelines to follow?

First of all, I believe the process of becoming an instant grandparent should not be hurried. There has to be ample time to learn to know each new child who has come into your life. It is not the same as with the announcement of your own grandchildren. There is no time of preparation: no time to witness the growth within the womb: no time to knit the booties: no time to eagerly anticipate that precious day of birth when you inherit the sweetest name on earth—Grandma!

THE ART OF GRANDPARENTING

Suddenly they are just there! In my case, my new grandchildren ranged in ages at the time of our marriage from two to sixteen. Based on their age level and personalities, each one had their own opinions and feelings of their grandfather's remarriage. That, of course, also included their feelings toward me. How was I to react? How were they to react?

Common sense told me to go slow. I know now I probably over reacted early on. I expected these new grandchildren to display the same type of respectful behavior in my home that my own grandchildren had been taught to do. There were occasions when the younger ones really got on my nerves as they were allowed to go through the kitchen cupboards, jump on our bed, rearrange the table centerpiece. I was dumbfounded that their grandfather did not stop them and I did not know what my role in discipline was! I know now I should have learned to be more tolerant. These were children who had been brought up differently. Obviously, those things just weren't considered disrespectful in their own grandmother's home. (Many of you instant grandma readers out there may know just what I am talking about—and maybe some of you who are not so instant!) Let me just say that these children are older now and have developed into sophisticated, beautiful human beings. I just wish we could have gotten off to a better start. If I had to deal with that part of my journey again I would try to just look the other way, even if it meant I had to grit my teeth and bite my tongue. I also discussed my feeling with my husband, though he did not think I should be so upset.

With the older ones I found it necessary to stand back and let nature take its course for the first year or so. I did not try to force attention or expect them to give any. I did try hard to get to know them by asking about their school activities, their involvement with sports, etcetera. As the sense of trust grew, the barriers slowly broke down and a gradual acceptance began to take place.

With the two-year-old it was altogether different. Because

she was so young, she never had the opportunity to know her real grandma before she died, so she instantly took to me and was the only one who readily addressed me as "Grandma." Of course, I loved it and took every opportunity to play my part. Those feelings may change as she grows older and learns I am not her real grandma. It will be interesting to see how it goes.

During this time of getting to know each other, I understood above everything else the importance of never, ever trying to take the place of the real grandmother. Actually, it would have been the most disrespectable action I could have taken. NOBODY takes the place of a dearly bereaved relative. That much I knew. There had to be another approach to winning these kids over: some other way of earning their trust of this new woman on the block.

Of course, my husband and I had discussed some things prior to combining our families and both of us agreed we should proceed with caution, not trying to move in too quickly with our newly acquired grandchildren. We both agreed we would continue to be singly, financially responsible in remembering birthdays, Christmas, graduation gifts, contributing to college expenses, etc. for our own blood grandchildren. However, it seemed proper the gift be acknowledged using both our names: for his children we sign the gift from Grandpa Monroe and Carol and for mine just the opposite, from Grandma Carol and Monroe. This has proved to work fantastically well. We also share attending their school functions, weddings, graduations, and so on, together as much as possible. Upon occasion there has been a conflict in which two functions have been at the same time in which case it is understood that he will attend his grandchild's function and I go to my own grandchild's.

There was, the first year we were married, also the problem of what to do with our kids and grandkids at holiday times. Both sides of our families had been used to going to the grandparents' homes for the major holidays: Thanksgiving, Christmas, Easter. All we could come up with that first year was to give the invitation to both sides of the family and whoever could come was welcome. Well, that proved to be a bit overwhelming considering many of them *could* come, probably as much out of curiosity as anything else, to see how this thing was going to work! Well, we discovered quickly that our modest-sized town home simply does not accommodate forty or more people, so after that we came up with the idea that we would alternate families: mine would come for Christmas one year and his would come for Thanksgiving, with the kids opening their own homes for the ones they would not spend with us. Then the next year it would be switched. This seems to work pretty well. As of recent, we have started purchasing ready-made meals when the gang comes: barbecued spare ribs and fried chicken are favorites. Everybody seems to enjoy this and it makes life so much easier.

Learning to accept the good times along with the bad is all part of the game. We try to hold each other up at such times when life deals a bad hand. His grandchildren's problems have become mine and vice-versa, as it should be. On the other side of the coin we also share their joys and accomplishments. When I was blessed at age seventy with the birth of a new granddaughter, and three months later the birth of my first great-granddaughter we both delighted in welcoming these new additions to our family. We also later both mourned the death of his first great-grandchild, a beautiful little girl who lived only a few short hours after birth.

I remember well the time we were visiting the home of my husband's oldest daughter. Their second son was born with a type of autism which limits his ability to interact socially with people. This is a normal reaction with autistic children and I must say his parents have done an awesome job in raising him. Today he is an accomplished artist and on his way to success. One of these non-

THE ART OF GRANDPARENTING

sociable traits is his extreme honesty in expressing whatever comes to mind at any particular time, something the rest of us have to stifle! This means that he generally says what he thinks and feels. On this particular occasion he bluntly said aloud to me in the presence of others: "Carol, you are a nice lady but you just aren't my Grandma Delma."

I was not really shocked, partly because of my educational background in Special Education in which I worked with a variety of special-needs children and was well grounded in accepting 'out of the blue' comments, but mostly because I felt prepared in the response I had ready for him. I saw it as an opportunity to talk to him openly as well as to others in the presence within hearing range. First, I asked him to tell me all about his Grandma because I never knew her. This got him to open up and focus on our conversation. Then I simply explained I would never be able to take the place of his real grandmother any more than his own grandfather would be able to completely fill the space left with the death of my own grandchildren's dear grandfather. That would simply not be our goal. Rather we wished to be friends and try to fill in maybe just a bit, knowing it would be somewhat different from having his real grandma, or in my case my grandchildren having their real grandpa. I believe it helped in explaining it this way because he obviously had not given thought to the other side of the coin. Also, I explained that we hoped it made them all happy to realize his grandpa and I loved each other very much and wanted to take care of each other in this world. Being lonesome is not a good thing and neither his grandpa nor I were lonesome anymore. His response, "Pass the chocolate," led me to believe he had been satisfied with my profound speech. My comparison rating with his Grandma Delma was never challenged again.

At a later date when he was in my home there was a debate as to the brand of chocolate I kept in the refrigerator. Thinking it would be not so good I told him to, "Just try it," attached with the words, "Just trust me on this." With bated breath I waited. Finally, along came the answer from him as he scooped the last bit from the dish, "Carol, you were right. I think my grandpa married the right person." Whew!

Not everyone will have opportunity to be caught off guard as I was, but the point I am trying to make is the necessity of having a mind set early on as to your own true expectations. It certainly makes the journey less complicated when you know yourself where you are headed. In situations where there are no guidelines it is necessary to use common sense and develop some! In some sense it compares to trying to take a trip without following the directions of a map. It can be disastrous!

There was another occasion before we were married in which an older granddaughter of my husband-to-be let her feelings be known. Shortly after she learned about our relationship, she made it clear by her actions that she did not approve one bit. For example, she turned my picture upside down in her grandpa's living room. She thought her grandfather was being unfaithful by getting engaged to some woman so soon after her grandmother had died.

I had never met this sixteen-year-old girl, and when the time finally came to meet her, she was very standoffish and aloof. It was difficult to know just how to handle the situation because I didn't know her that well. When we got the opportunity to be alone I decided to approach her actions head on. She was old enough to understand what I was saying, so I talked to her on an adult level. Basically, I told her why we wanted to get married and that in no way was it meant to show disrespect to either of our deceased spouses. She seemed to warm a little, even though our relationship has never developed into a real close one. I have learned one thing from this experience: people will make their own choices, and no matter how hard you wish for their approval, there will always be those who walk to the beat of a different drummer. My only bit of advice is to go on with life. What else are you supposed to do? In the meantime, I see no point in worrying about this. I do not believe that anyone needs to beat themselves up over something that they need not take a guilt trip for in the first place. I do think as she has matured she has become less judgmental and is doing a better job of accepting things as they are.

Lest the reader think that the journey has all been full of potholes, let me tell about some of the happy times along the way. There were concerts and high school musicals performed by the high school age girls that we both attended. There were graduation exercises and art showings. There was a baptism. There have been numerous holiday and birthday celebrations. There was the time when we stayed for a few days with a couple of his granddaughters while their parents went to Europe on an anniversary trip.

As the years go by, the barriers seem to break down little by little. No, I will never be their Grandma Delma. On the other hand, they will never be my own grandchildren. My husband will never be my own grandchildren's Grandpa Leo. They will never be his own grandchildren. What we must remember is that none of this was planned this way. It has happened for better or for worse. I believe everybody wants it to be for the better. We are blessed with Christian families on both sides and we all know what is right and acceptable in God's sight. As a result I am learning to love these new grandkids that have come into my life. No, it will never be the same sort of relationship I have with my own blood grandchildren. That just can't be, and understanding that is perfectly, naturally okay.

I have learned many lessons so far along this journey. Juggling two families is not an easy task. Several times I have almost reached the breaking point—two Thanksgivings, two Christmases, two Easters,

THE ART OF GRANDPARENTING

two Fourth of July's which are expected of me to celebrate when I am dog tired from the first one! It is at these times that I go to my Father and ask for strength. He has promised He will not give us more than we can bear, and sometimes when we have reached that point it is up to us to say, "No more." I am finding myself saying, "No!" more frequently as my body ages. Why should we push ourselves into a state of anxiety? I pass this advice along to bring comfort to the minds of all of you who feel you have to be all things to all people at all times. Learn to listen to your body and say that word, "No!" when necessary.

In summary, becoming a grandmother without even trying is not for wimps! It takes the patience of Job, the Wisdom of Solomon, and the love of Jesus. Bringing two families together is one of the hardest things I have ever had to deal with in this world. I am still learning and expect to be until I tell this world good-bye. But, I know with love in charge and patience at the helm, things can fall into place. No, it will never be the same again. It doesn't take a rocket scientist to figure that out. But in spite of all, try to remember that these beautiful new people who have come into your lives deserve the best. Welcome the challenge and go forth with confidence.

the Art of Grandparenting

Tips & Tricks

Don't hurry into becoming a grandparent with the new grandchildren. Take it slowly. Get to know them.

Be tolerant of how the new grandchildren were brought up differently from your blood-related grandchildren.

With older grandchildren, stand back and let nature take its course for the first year or so, trying not to force attention or expect them to give any.

Accept the good times along with the bad as part of the game.

Accept that you will not replace another grandparent.

Learn to listen to your body and say that word, "No!" when necessary.

Remember that these beautiful new people who have come into your lives deserve the best.

Worn Out Nostalgia

Bob Kascht

The day for which you have waited is approaching. Are you ready? Expectation is not the same as advance preparation. Women must do sweet little fussy things like preparing a second hope chest with treasured remnants of their past. They assemble recipes to share. Folk wisdoms that never really worked are repackaged and issued with proper solemnity. They twitter and act like a secret sisterhood of the temple, knowing all about the wonders of birth. These are grandmothers in waiting. They know it will be a girl.

Men, with their macho bravado, don't bother much. They are secure, knowing they can manage anything that is required. Of course, they have the fishing tackle ready, and the baseball glove softened up because they feel it in their bones, it is going to be a boy.

Becoming a grandparent is the ultimate stage in the continuum of living. It is the official biologic and cultural pronouncement that one has completed the cycle of creation. It is a fulfillment and a promise. Although this seems to be an automatic succession, focused sensitive effort is needed to bring out the many nuances of this complex blending of gene pools: a miraculous new being.

The Art of Grandparenting

Just a few cautionary comments about grandchildren. You have been looking forward to them, with expectations of repeating your interactions with your own grandparents, but it may not actually come off that way. Your grandchildren are alive in the real world, a place that is different from what you know. It is technologically dominated, and though you try your best, you cannot feel spontaneously comfortable in it. You have had to learn to use your computer, cell phone, blackberry, and even a DVD, but for them it is instinctive, as natural and reflex as a beating heart. They are an integral product of TODAY, while you flit between two worlds, from a half-remembered, idealized past into their world which, you hope is like yours, but you must remember they have no past. You are their link to what came before them, and you must recreate it for them, although many times it will seem that you are forcing it, and they are reluctant or disinterested. This age presents a greater disconnect than probably any previous generation gap because of the cyber-speed with which things happen, not allowing time to adapt.

You may expect that this is like parenting, a natural continuum, and hope to feel instincts that will guide you. Not so. You are a supernumerary, carried along gratuitously. If you want a role more prominent than just a walk-on part, you will have to write the scenario yourself. This is quite unlike your grandparents' part staged in a simpler universe. In the microcosm of the farm, or even in the sameness of a small town, we were inescapably together every day. Certainly, I was often in the way, but my grandparents learned to expect me to be there and to do something. Eventually, that became my duty, my contribution to our survival plan. Some of my most penetrating memories are the result of things that miscarried,—like the time Grandpa Frank let me operate the spark lever on the Model T while he hand-cranked it to start. My timing was somewhat off, and the crank handle kicked in reverse and broke his wrist. I was for

THE ART OF GRANDPARENTING

a moment of time out of favor, but I learned that grandparents must be very forgiving.

When I was seven, my father became sick and that put an end to all the things we might have done together. I don't remember any special fuss or big talk about how things would still be all right, but Grandpa was just there and kept me going and growing. I knew he could do anything, except he never played baseball with me. I ran around the farm, free and happy, and survived not having a dad. Grandma fitted into this substitute pattern, made cookies, and did the little soft and huggy things. Grandparents were the padding that gave roundness and substance to my world just by being there, independent of the activities and events. I grew up with a warm sense that life was good.

Because I had such very limited time with my father, I resolved in my parenting to be a perfect dad, although I was without a model to follow. I was going to be interesting to my children. If my real activities hadn't been interesting, I made them so. I fantasized and fabricated. It was somewhat like Tom Sawyer painting the picket fence. Ordinary things took on a shine and glamour that was appealing. I consoled my deceitful self with a quote from Mark Twain: "When I was young I could remember everything, whether it happened or not.".

The grandparents of today live in a different paradigm from the one they hold in syrupy memory. It is frighteningly dynamic, often unfamiliar, even threatening. The traditional rewards of grandparenthood are not guaranteed. Respect and affection must be earned. Flexibility is essential if one is to adapt to the unfamiliar array of technology. Breezy, impersonal electronic communication exchanges have replaced the hug and handshake. Today's grandparents with a long memory can compare this to the impact of the shockingly irreverent flapper kiss-off "OH YOU KID" in a bygone era.

The Art of Grandparenting

When I had children, I didn't waste much time thinking about what to do next. It was mostly what had to be done, like putting one foot in front of the other. I didn't have a model and probably I wasn't at my best with diapers or a bottle, but I knew I was going to perform world class when they got old enough for a lecture, maybe at four or five. We all survived in reasonable peace and love. They grew and learned, in the seamless continuum of living, became mature and had their own children. It was time now for me to blossom. I had waited, unknowingly storing up all the riches of nostalgia from my childhood and my own parenting, eager to share wonders with the tender and receptive youngsters who were presented to me. Mary had her own checklist of what a grandmother is, and readied to be a reincarnation of all her most cherished memories. So we waited together, excitedly discussing strategies, plans for adventures, wonderful bits to be implanted, and love to flavor each day.

With each family addition we reviewed the scenario of our master plan. Mary even baked cookies, a few times. I tried to find a common ground with the teenagers, to prove I was once one of them. I shared my recall with them, real or imaginary, and strove to be interesting, tirelessly inventing episodes and scenes. At age twelve, I used to play my harmonica on the radio once a week, doing phone-in requests from the shut-ins. As a spin-off from this, I occasionally got a job playing at business banquets. I was definitely for the economy market. On one such occasion I played for the Iowa Druggist Association. I was paid only four crummy dollars, but that was where I got the idea to make up a story for our kids about having advised Charlie Walgreen to build separate stores and stay out of malls so he wasn't locked into sharing the misfortunes of others in the neighborhood who might be failing. I also drew on my sweetest memory as a soda jerk, and urged him to return ice-cream fountains and juke boxes. I referred the little people in my family audience to

THE ART OF GRANDPARENTING

reference this on Happy Days and Leave It to Beaver. I thought this replay of my teenaged coolness was pretty much guaranteed to win the grandkids. It didn't make it.

In one especially glowing and heartfelt performance, I elaborated on my influence on Sam Peoples. In my version, I probably was responsible for the development of the Federal Reserve Bank and our entire fiscal system. Sam was a worthy, honest, hardworking boy who supported his ailing mother with a paper route, was an A student and also an altar boy. When he was about to enter college, they raised the tuition by thirty dollars, and Sam didn't have the money, so I paid it. He continued on, earned an MBA and founded a bank. This was just the beginning of his empire. In later years, when we were driving on our vacations, I had the opportunity to point out to the family how many PEOPLE'S BANKS there were around the country. The awesome thing was I had a little part in making it all possible.

Sometime I sensed a little impatience. It was as if the grandchildren weren't getting as much out of these discussions as I was. I actually prepared for these sessions. My favorite Walter Mitty image of myself was a professor, maybe even an Oxford Don. I bought a smoking jacket at the *GOING OUT OF BUSINESS* sale at a Sullivan's men store. It had been marked down twice, probably because not many men in our town thought of themselves as being Walter Pidgeon or David Niven. Anyway, it was beautiful, maroon velvet with ribbed black silk lapels and piping on the pocket edges. In my reverie, I would sit in front of the fireplace, leather-bound book in hand, and read great wisdom to the little ones sprawled around me, wide-eyed, hanging on every word. All of this had some magic until they reached twelve. I don't know if that was when they discovered the opposite sex, or when they got new laptops and blackberries. Anyway, I never developed the same rapport that I had with grandpa Frank when we were sitting in the barn milking and squirting at the cat.

THE ART OF GRANDPARENTING

The present situation is something of a coexistent truce. I still call them, and they still come to visit, but the ground rules are a little different. I don't try to dazzle them. I am just pleading for them to show me how to straighten out a quirk in my computer or text with my thumbs. They are most patient and tolerant, and always kiss us goodbye as they rush off to some essential activity. I think we have rationalized a moral from all of this, something like: "half a loaf is better than none." We greatly love them, and know they will visit us in the nursing home.

The rubric truths of this relationship shine through the clutter of words, worthy of being accepted as commandments, but the guiding theme is simple love. With that dominating the climate, all else falls into proper perspective. Be patient, undemanding, non-judgmental and accessible. You don't have to be perfect and saintly. Just be yourself, but be consistent. Your values, and your individual flavor, are the essence of what the grandchildren will identify with your memory for all time. Don't impose your ideas or wishes merely to be in control or for your own pleasure. Realize that you are something of a refuge from the authoritarian role of their parents, but don't be maneuvered or exploited. Remember how you assembled the image of your grandparents from many, little, uneventful, day to day doings, until this grew into the larger than life memory that you are now trying to duplicate. Be respectfully aware that grandparenthood is usually shared with another couple, but do not compete for popularity. Don't pander. Have realistic expectations. Enjoy vicariously the wonders of discovery as life unfolds for the little ones, until one day they drive up and introduce their new one and only, and the whole process starts over. If, in the real world, things don't follow this idealized scenario, you can always bake a few cookies, or go fishing.

the Art of Grandparenting

Tips & Tricks

Respect and affection must be earned.

Flexibility is essential if one is to adapt to the unfamiliar array of technology.

Find your own way to build a rapport, even if it isn't sitting in the barn squirting cow's milk at the cat, or baking cookies, or going fishing.

Realize that you offer escape from the rules of their parents, but avoid being maneuvered or exploited. Have some rules of your own.

Remember, they have other grandparents who love them as you do. No popularity contests are in order.

Even though you know you are not perfect, be patient, undemanding, non-judgmental and accessible.

Just be yourself, but be consistent.

Be careful about developing expectations, and don't buy a smoking jacket for story-telling sessions.

Love is the dominant theme that puts everything else in perspective.

Grandparents, Tell Your Story

Irene Watson

As grandparents, one of the greatest gifts we can give our grandchildren is to tell them who we are, to let them know us. We don't have to be stereotypical old people who ramble. We can tell our stories with focus and meaning, imparting pearls of wisdom; our stories can serve as examples of how to live and what mistakes to avoid; they can instill courage in our grandchildren, helping them to confront their own challenges and learn resilience; our stories become hope for future generations.

You may think your grandchildren are too young to care, understand, or listen to you. Don't let that stop you from telling your story. You may never have thought about how important that story is and will be. I intend to convert you into becoming a storyteller, and then I'll provide a few suggestions for how to do it effectively.

Besides writing down my own story in the form of my memoir (more about that later), for many years, I have been an avid genealogist. The first step people take in researching their family tree is to talk to the family elders—the grandparents, great-aunts and great-uncles—asking them what they remember about their own parents and grandparents. While the researcher gets some information, time and again they hear Aunt Edna or Grandpa Johnson say, "My father (mother, grandmother, grandfather) used to tell me about the family, but I was just a kid so I didn't really listen; now I wish I had paid more attention." Stories were lost, partly because the receiver did not pay attention, partly because they were not written down. What we wouldn't give today to get those stories back! My point is that your story does matter; even if you don't think it matters today, it will matter immensely to your children and grandchildren in the future. It will be a priceless treasure for generations to come.

"But I didn't do anything really important in my life," you might say. But you did. You lived. You had a human experience. You touched countless other lives in large and small ways, in ways you will never fully know. Little things you mention that you might not even think important could matter immensely to your descendants, providing them a sense of belonging, a sense of identity. Let me give a couple of examples:

A couple adopts a child. They love the child, feed and clothe him, nurture him, and never let him want for anything. Let's say the father is a logger and the mother a nurse. Their son, however, grows up to be an English teacher. There are no teachers in the family; no one even cares to read much. Years later, the birth mother looks up her son. She's a newspaper editor. He got his love for reading, writing and language from his birth mother—he may have spent his life feeling he didn't quite fit in with his adopted family, only to find his birth family shares his interests. What a treasure for him to understand where his traits or interests come from.

One of my friends was the only member of his family who liked to write stories. One day his great-aunt gave him some old family papers. He was stunned to find among them some short stories his great-grandmother and his great-great grandfather wrote. He was exuberant to discover he came from a line of storytellers; it gave him a strengthened sense of identity and a resolve to keep writing. Today he's published several novels.

Our ancestors shape our lives. There's no getting away from it. Telling our story helps those who come after us understand both themselves and us. If anyone understands that, it's me, as I'll now explain by telling a little of my own story.

My Story and Why I Told It

My memoir, *The Sitting Swing*, tells the story of my recovery from the self-defeating behaviors I learned during an abusive childhood. To understand my family's dysfunction, I had to know my parents' story as well. Their story helped me to understand, sympathize with and ultimately forgive my parents, and it allowed my story to change for the better.

My parents were pioneers—not the nineteenth century American frontier type, but twentieth century Canadian pioneers. My grandparents took the chance at homesteading in Canada because life in Russia had become nearly impossible. First, they had been forced out of their village in Russia during the revolution; upon their return, they were given ten acres to divide among six children (as well as their families); that small amount of land could not support their farming needs, and land was being given away in Canada to those who would develop it.

In 1929, when my father was fourteen, the family traveled to Canada, first to Quebec City, and then on to northern Alberta, where they claimed the land they would call their own: Trees. That's all their land was—trees. My grandmother took one look and, like the stoic woman she had to be, uttered not a sound, but tears streamed down her face. They had given up very little in exchange for absolutely nothing. Nothing solid at least. But there was potential, so all they could do was go to work.

In a day, they had a shelter of sod and branches; that was where they slept, weathering thunderstorms and mosquitoes during the five weeks it took them to build a more permanent home—a 16'x20' log cabin. Everything was built by hand. Food was cooked over an open fire.

As winter started to settle in, the little money they had was petering out. They didn't know what to expect of an Alberta winter. They had no notion they could face temperatures of forty to fifty degrees below zero for days at a time. They were shocked into the harshest facts of their new reality when their cache of potatoes froze inside their house and went to waste.

Walking miles to school through many feet of snow is the stereotypical martyr's speech, isn't it? But that's exactly what happened. My father and his younger brothers walked about three miles to school every day through Alberta's unkind winters and on into spring. And the school was taught in English. They knew barely a word of the language, but they learned. They couldn't accomplish much in their new land otherwise. My dad made it through the third grade before he quit towork on the farm. By then, he was sixteen. No more time for education nonsense.

Somehow they managed, even though the entire land had to be cleared before they could farm it. They couldn't harvest their first crop for two years, but somehow they got along.

When my dad was twenty-seven, he was able to afford his own parcel of land. He moved out of his parents' home and into a two-room house he built himself.

You can see why I'd grant my father an individualized view of the world—*his* world *was* extreme and born of necessities—food, shelter, warmth. Education and self-actualization weren't on his chart. He was struggling with the basics.

The Art of Grandparenting

My mom also went to school and matched my dad's educational level by achieving third grade. By then, she was fourteen—that was plenty of education for a woman. So she began working as a maid and nanny for a wealthy family.

My parents met about the time my father bought his own land. The two-room home he built was for his bride-to-be, my mother, sixteen when they married. He was twenty-seven.

As the final ingredient in the family background that shaped who I became, my brother, Alexander, was born. My mother was seventeen at the time, even then a bit young to give birth to a child. My mom was certain her age made the difference in Alexander's health—he was born underweight and sickly. He had colic and dysentery at the same time. He had rectal bleeding. And she—my mother—got blamed.

The women of the community came to help. They offered a great deal of support. They offered their wisdom, but wisdom centered on blaming Alexander's illness on my mother's youth. Ultimately, my mother came to blame herself for my brother's death.

My parents had a difficult life—the loss of their child was devastating to them; they were terrified by the thought that they might also lose me. My mother compensated by being over-protective, controlling who I could play with, barely allowing me out of her sight, not even wanting me to think for myself. Today I understand why my parents behaved the way they did, although it took a long time for me to grow past the strict and even abusive upbringing I had. I resented them for years once I escaped from their tyranny. But it was by knowing their story, by putting my family events into perspective years later that I was able to make my peace and forgive them.

By telling my story, I hope my children and grandchildren, and many other readers will find strength to tell their own. Stories matter. They inspire. They encourage. They heal.

THE ART OF GRANDPARENTING

So now that you know my story, let's get on with you telling yours.

What We Can Learn From Family History

My story is about recovery and overcoming dysfunction. Yours might be as well, or maybe you did a good job raising your children—you didn't mess them up too much anyway. Hopefully, you don't need to tell your story from a need to justify your decisions or actions to your children and grandchildren, but you must have things you want to share with them regardless—things about yourself, things about your parents and grandparents—stories about family members you remember who are no longer able to tell their stories, but who had stories you want to preserve.

Think about how many stories the human family has had to tell, and how many have never been told.

Have you ever thought about how many ancestors you have? You have two parents, four grandparents, and eight great-grandparents. Each generation back, the number doubles. By the time you get to your eleven-greats grandparents, you have 8,384 ancestors in that generation, and seven more generations back to the eighteen-greats-grandparents, puts that generation's number over one million. However, the numbers don't consistently double after that, but instead, ancestors start repeating themselves because families intermarried—fifth cousins, often first cousins, married each other.

In truth, the human family is quite small, despite the millions of people who preceded us. DNA researchers have proven that anyone of European descent alive today is descended from anyone who lived in Europe and had children before 1200 A.D. That means every white person alive is descended from Charlemagne, Alfred the

The Art of Grandparenting

Great, William the Conqueror, Frederick Barbarossa and Eleanor of Aquitaine. If we go back not too many generations prior to that, white people will find they have ancestors from Asia and Africa, and Africans and Asians will find they have European ancestors.

Our grandchildren, by having an understanding of our stories and the mixture of people they came from, can learn that issues of race, culture and ethnicity—issues our ancestors slaughtered each other over—are really senseless because today we're a mixture of all those people and cultures. Europeans have the blood of Chinese fishermen and Indian farmers and Egyptian pharaohs in them. There really is no such thing as race—we're all part of the same human family.

If each one of your ancestors had told his or her story so it would be preserved for future generations, you could never read them all in a lifetime, yet how many of their stories do you really know? If you have written records from just one or two of them, you can consider yourself fortunate. But why were they so silent? Were they too busy? Were they unable to write? Did they think their lives didn't matter?

In the United States and Canada, many of us are only second or third generation descendants from immigrants. Our grandparents or great-grandparents came to North America, leaving the old world behind, often fleeing war, poverty, or oppression.

Many of those immigrants were stoic and silent about their pasts. Perhaps they didn't think anyone could understand or relate to their stories; many wanted to forget the past and start over, focusing on the future. But what stories they could have told us. They were the heroes of their generation—brave enough to seek out a better world where perhaps they would struggle, but where they had faith that life would be better for their children and grandchildren. Today we are blessed with the fruit of their labors, often not having the slightest idea of the great sacrifices they made for us. Think of what we could learn from their stories—of great-great-grandmother's account of

THE ART OF GRANDPARENTING

living through the Great Potato Famine, or the sacrifices Grandpa made so his family could survive the Great Depression.

Those stories are what family is about—the family stories that survive help shape the family identity, giving us a sense of who we are, and providing us strength; if our ancestors survived against such Herculean odds, then we can carry on as well.

WHO ARE YOUR GRANDCHILDREN?

Remember how everyone of European descent alive today is descended from every European who lived before the year 1200 A.D.? Project yourself into the future. Provided your grandchildren produce children and so on, by the year 3,000 A.D. you will be ancestor to most if not all of the human race. If you have any question about how important it is to tell your story, that should speak volumes. Ancestor to the human race! You can't get any more important than that.

When we think of descendants, we think of bloodlines, but that's not always true if children have been adopted in our families. Bloodlines don't matter as much as the inheritance of culture. Your legacy is the gift you leave future generations. Author and poet Maya Angelou has no daughters, yet she wrote *Letters to My Daughters* to impart her wisdom and life experiences to future generations. There's no reason why you can't do the same. Think of George Washington or Thomas Jefferson. You may not be descended from them, but the legacies they left have enriched the lives of Americans for more than two centuries. You can do the same by telling your story. Maybe you were never President of the United States, but you have wisdom and life experiences that need to be shared.

We are a link in the great chain of being, in the expanding, unfolding human story, not just by blood but by influence. What we say, think and do is the legacy of the future human race.

THE ART OF GRANDPARENTING

We Personally Benefit from Telling Our Story

If I haven't yet convinced you to tell your story for your grandchildren, tell it for your own sake. When we tell our story, we also listen to it, and we revise it, changing our perspective on who we are.

In writing *The Sitting Swing*, I gained new insights about myself. My memories were like pieces of a jigsaw puzzle I had to put together. First I found similar pieces, like you would match colors to find out which puzzle pieces will connect; I took pieces of my life and turned them into sections of my life that became chapters in my book. Then I connected those sections to each other to create a complete picture, an entire book. In doing so, I found the patterns from which I could make sense and meaning for myself.

By telling ourselves our story, we reshape it; we revise it. To revise is to do a re-vision, to see it again. When we see it again, we can put it into context; we can see how one event in our lives was shaped by the events that preceded it, and how that event influenced important decisions we made later.

Sometimes this aspect of telling our story can be frightening. We revisit parts of the past we might prefer to forget, but more often than not, we go back to those events and find they made us stronger. Bad experiences probably had the greatest effect on shaping who we are; now we become thankful, if not for the experience, for the growth it inspired. Or perhaps we find, in telling our story, that the picture isn't as rosy as we would like—we have regrets; we fear we weren't a good parent. Maybe we made mistakes, but we still have time to learn from those mistakes. We can compensate by being wonderful grandparents, and in the process, also become closer to our children. We retell our story, changing "I was a bad parent" to

THE ART OF GRANDPARENTING

"I am a wonderful, fun, loving grandparent." We feel better about ourselves, we rejuvenate our lives, we make the future hopeful. We wake up, like Ebenezer Scrooge on Christmas morning, realizing the ghost of the past can lead us into a new and hopeful future.

How to Begin the Storytelling Process

There are many ways to tell your story. It doesn't have to be simply by talking—be prepared that your grandchildren may not want to listen, and if they do listen, they may only be humoring you. Don't leave your legacy solely in the hands of a thirteen-year old granddaughter who's more interested in teenage boys than Grandpa's Vietnam War experience. Oral stories are wonderful, and they can be a great way to bond with your grandchildren, but create a lasting record as well.

Here are a few simple ways to tell your story:

Tips & Tricks

Get out the old photographs.

If you're like most people, you probably have hundreds of photographs not in albums, or in albums but not labeled. Collect all those photographs; put them in albums and identify the people in the pictures and the dates when they were taken. If you're high-tech, scan them onto a computer. Ask a grandchild to help you—what a wonderful bonding experience to have—to teach your grandchild her family history while she teaches you modern technology. Don't be afraid. Your grandchild will know what she's doing with that computer. You supply the photographs and memories, and she'll figure out how to organize and preserve them. In the process, be sure to take photographs of the two of you working together, and of everything going forward in your life so the story continues.

Start keeping a journal.

It doesn't have to be a daily history of your life. A notebook, a word document on the computer—anything that works for you. Commit to writing in it daily, even if just for ten minutes. You don't have to record each day's events. Maybe you want to start each page with "I remember..." On day one, you can tell about something you and a friend did in the fourth grade; the next day, write about the day you were married, and the next day, recall your fiftieth birthday. Don't worry about chronology—you can rearrange it all later. If you've already been keeping a journal for years, maybe this is the time to take those old paper diaries, find the keys, and unlock them for future generations. Start typing them up on the computer before the paper crumbles and the ink fades. This is also your chance to control your story—I don't mean to lie about your life, but we all occasionally do things we'd rather other people did not know. You have a chance to edit yourself a bit before the next generation gets their hands on those confessions you wrote in your diary about your schoolgirl crush.

Write your memoirs.

This kind of writing may be more chronological and orderly than your journal, and it's a bit more ambitious, but do what works best for you. If you're really creative, write it in third person; write it as a novel with yourself as the lead character. Think about what the conflicts were in your life, and who were the main characters. Is there a theme to your life? Is there a message you want to convey about what you, the main character, learned as a result of your experiences?

Make a recording

This is easier for many people than writing things down. Ask a family member to interview you; don't worry about how you sound on tape—just make sure the tape doesn't shut off while you're still talking. What a treasure it will be for future generations to hear your voice telling your story in your own words. And if you don't like your voice, you can always transcribe the tape to paper later.

There's no wrong way to tell your story. It's your story. It's completely yours and completely unique. You get to decide how to tell it. Just get started doing it. You owe it to future generations, but most of all, you owe it to yourself.

Knocked Sideways by Love

Barbara Abercrombie

I was not a mother who hinted to her daughters to get pregnant so I could have grandchildren. Frankly, becoming a grandmother sounded a little old to me. My own grandmothers, bless their hearts, were always old. They wore old lady shoes and dresses, and I believe one even wore a hairnet on occasion. They were always going to the doctor and they moved slowly and carefully. When they were around me they were cautious, anxious, and stern. While I loved them, I didn't want to become them. And I found my friends who had recently become grandparents extremely boring in their need to incessantly share photographs of small babies and toddlers and relate their recent bons mots. Icky was a word that often came to mind.

It wasn't that I did not not want to become a grandmother, (not that I had any say in the matter) but it just wasn't high on my agenda. I had recently remarried, was busy writing and teaching, and as I turned sixty I still felt too young to acquire the title Grandmother. But if it did happen, I intended to be an incredibly cool grandmother and slightly aloof. I'd love my grandchildren of course, but I'd remain very much involved in my own life, I wouldn't get all kissy face and

THE ART OF GRANDPARENTING

huggy with them and flash around a lot of their photographs to my friends or post them on a Facebook page.

One August afternoon visiting my daughter Brooke in her kitchen as she was making sauce from the tomatoes in her garden, she casually announced that she thought she was a few weeks pregnant. To my surprise I burst into tears of joy. It turned out she was indeed pregnant. When we saw the first sonogram of the baby and learned it was a girl, tears of joy flowed again. A girl! Since I'd had girls of my own I secretly believed that girl babies were the best babies, and I realized that nothing could be more wonderful than to have my first grandchild be a girl. I pinned my copy of the photo of this little tadpole who was about to become my granddaughter above my computer. Her parents chose the name Emma for her. She was like a guest from far, far away who was coming to visit the following April, and we all began to get ready for her. God help me, I even started knitting.

Among her four prospective grandparents there was much discussion over what we wanted Emma to call us. Some of our choices were: M'Dear, Captain, Papa, and variations of charming foreign words for grandparent. None of us chose a name prefixed with Grand (not in English anyway); no one wanted to be called Grandma or Grandpa. We were all too young.

And then came April 5th, the day before my own birthday, and Emma arrived. "How's that for a birthday present!" said Brooke, and I had to admit it was the best birthday present I'd ever gotten. But here's what I didn't realize would happen: I fell in love. I didn't know how momentous—as in earth standing still, oceans roaring, heart soaring—it would feel to hold my own granddaughter less than an hour after her birth. I didn't realize I'd fall madly in love with her instantly. I mean crazed song lyric type love. I just wanted to hold her, be with her all the time. Of course I had believed that I'd like her

THE ART OF GRANDPARENTING

a lot, and eventually love her, but never had I imagined that I'd fall in love like this. That I'd be knocked sideways by love.

I moved into Brooke's house for a week to help out when they got home from the hospital a few days later. I'd sit for hours in the rocking chair in the nursery holding Emma—looking into her face, seeing the future, really seeing it for the first time in my life. And also seeing the past. I thought of all the faces in her family—her other grandparents, her aunts and uncles, her great-grandparents. I thought of her great-great-grandparents, my own grandparents, those dear grandmas of mine, who were born in the 1800's. I thought of all the nationalities and the races that combined to bring Emma to us. The miracle of a new generation.

Loving Emma left me inarticulate. And I realized that when love was this pure it didn't need words or explanations, it just was. So I held her close and rocked her hour after hour in the same chair I had once rocked her mother and aunt. Her expressions, half smiles and yawns, sudden squinting red-faced rage from hunger pangs were infinitely interesting to me. As well as the sounds she made, little coos and grunts and startled noises that sounded like "Ahah!"—as if she'd just figured something out. Her face was the color of honey and peaches, her mouth was perfect, her eyes were ocean colored, she had her father's long fingers, her mother's chin. She smelled like clean laundry and flowers.

When my daughters were little I created a rigid schedule in order to get my writing done, but now all schedules, except for teaching one class a week, fell by the wayside. If Brooke needed back up care, I'd jump in my car, hit the freeway and head to her house, day or night. When Emma was eighteen months old we began going to

THE ART OF GRANDPARENTING

Mommy and Me Yoga together every Thursday morning. Emma insisted on dressing herself for the yoga class. Always in layers: sweat pants, t-shirts, a couple of dresses, and different colored socks, plus a hat or two. She looked like a miniature bag lady.

When I told one of my friends about her amazing outfits, my friend said, "But shouldn't you supervise or something?"

"Why?" I asked.

"So she'll learn how to dress properly," she said.

I shrugged. As a grandparent, proper was no longer in my vocabulary.

One day as Emma ran around our house naked after her bath she suddenly stopped, looked at me embarrassed, shouted, "whoops!" and proceeded to pee on the Oriental rug in the bedroom. I told her it was okay and mopped it up. When her mother and aunt were little girls their father and I called our living room—and it embarrasses me to admit this—the *No No Room*. During the day they couldn't play in the living room and in the evening if there were adults in the room they could come in but not put their feet on the furniture or bring in any toys that might mess things up. The room was full of that awful faux Spanish furniture of the nineteen sixties and yards of wall to wall beige carpeting—all of it pretty ugly and very sterile. But it was a time in my life when the only thing I could feel in control of was the cleanliness and total order of this one room. If my daughters had peed on the beige carpet in the *No No Room* I'm afraid all hell would have broken loose. Now I have slipcovers that can be thrown in the washing machine if little people walk barefoot with dirty feet over the couches and chairs, and the beauty of Oriental rugs is that pee stains don't show.

A few years after Emma was born, my younger daughter Gillan became pregnant. With a boy. My first grandson was on his way and suddenly boy babies sounded just fine. More than fine—thrilling in fact. Axel arrived on a warm summer morning, and when he was fifteen minutes old, I saw him for the first time and dissolved into tears. I held him in my arms, looked into his fathomless blue eyes and lo and behold, I was in love.

Two years later Gillan was pregnant again. This time with a girl—to be named Grace, after my mother. I realized I wanted my third grandchild to have her own first for me; I already had First Grandchild and First Grandson, so I wondered, what could be a first for Grace? Finally I asked my daughter if I could be in the delivery room when she arrived; Grace could be my First Grandchild Seen Born. Gillan and the doctor agreed that I could be there, and on the day of her delivery my son-in-law and I were bundled up in paper scrubs to watch as Grace was born by caesarian section. I saw her come into this world. I saw the doctor pull this tiny precious creature into the light, a moment that can only be described as holy. There were six of us in the delivery room and then there were seven. This was the moment I got to share with Grace. And with Grace only.

Tears flowed and I was in love again. I know in theory the human heart can expand and hold more love than we ever think possible, but to experience this for a third time just knocked me sideways.

Over the years I've done a lot of thinking, not to mention talking, about love. I've read about love and I've written about love. I love my husband, my daughters, my extended family and close friends; but that love is based on history and shared values, years of talking and thousands of memories. That love grew. The love for grandchildren simply appeared; love at first sight. Of course I must have loved my daughters in this irrational, sudden way when they were babies. But when you're the mother you're much more into the daily nitty gritty

THE ART OF GRANDPARENTING

of care, nursing the baby, dealing with changes in your own body, and shifts in your relationship with the baby's father and your own parents. You're sleep deprived and scared and nervous. I was anyway. My daughters were born eleven months apart and my memories of those first years are sketchy at best. I had to keep them alive; I had to feed them and keep them clean and healthy and happy. I wanted to be a good mother, the best possible mother. Loving my grandchildren feels much more pure, less complicated, and at the same time filled with perspective.

The very word grandchildren always used to sound generic to me—like a small tribe of children who would more or less look alike and act alike. Other people's children and grandchildren seem to have this sameness, but not my own. The personalities of Emma, Axel and Grace are as developed and as different as a trio of fifty-year-old adults.

I've read articles about the necessity for grandmothers in hunter/gathering tribes, the idea that women beyond their childbearing years contributed to the survival of the tribe with their wisdom. One study believed that this is limited to maternal grandmothers (an idea I'm fond of quoting to my daughters at any given opportunity), but another study claims that older men as well as women have vital survival skills to pass on to the tribe. I'm still trying to come up with vital survival skills I might know to pass on to my grandchildren. How to boil an egg? Iron a shirt? Plant tomatoes? They already know the important stuff: how to be passionate about what they love, how to let curiosity consume them, how to be fearless and take risks.

But I really have no wisdom or advice to pass on to them or to other grandparents. All I have is this crazed love for three little people who are perfect. Their mothers and my husband—all of whom I'd walk on burning coals for if necessary—are much loved by me but they are not perfect. So maybe this is at the heart of being a grandparent. You can declare your grandchildren perfect. You can love them without an agenda, no matter how well meaning that agenda might be. There's no need for one. They are perfect just as they are.

I did not become the cool, aloof grandmother that I'd envisioned. I swoop into their houses and cover them with kisses, and sometimes if I'm busy I do drive-by hugs. My favorite thing in the world is to load up with Kettle Korn and G-rated movies, and invite them over for PJ parties. Emma calls me Babs, so all three now call me Babs and they call my husband Bobby — a name no one has ever called him before in his life.

And about those photographs people are always showing of their grandchildren? I've decided it's not at all icky. I have albums, whole albums, I'll show you at the drop of a hat. Or just check out my Facebook page.

Tips & Tricks

Even if you're sure you'll never whip out pictures of your grandchildren, buy the photo albums, and be sure to get a Facebook page!

Get ready to become a happily blithering idiot, babbling and cooing, staring and gooey-eyed at a little baby who just turned your life upside-down.

Schedules will fade. Rules will subside. Allow yourself to just *BE* in the moment, even if there is pee on the Oriental carpet. Nothing is so precious as a grandchild.

Love will stretch to knock you sideways for every grandchild you have. Grandchildren are perfect, and you can say so out loud!

Stories I'd Rather Not Tell

Hannah Yakin

Of all my twenty-three grandchildren, there is not one who doesn't stop short in his or her tracks when I put on my storytelling face and casually start: "When you were a little child...." Although I love to have an audience, there are stories I prefer not to tell. One of these concerns my very first experience as a grandmother, more than twenty-seven years ago.

Since my daughter-in-law was a new immigrant who had no relatives in Israel, I offered to help her out for a while after the birth of her first child. A day after the boy was born, I took a bus from Jerusalem to the Galilee where the young couple lived. When I arrived at their home, they had just kidnapped the baby from the maternity ward in Safed because a nurse wanted to take a drop of his blood for some routine tests. Apart from the urge they felt to fight the establishment tooth and nail, they were blissfully happy. If anything, my son regretted that he had just celebrated his nineteenth birthday, whereas he had hoped to beat the records in our family and become a father at eighteen. He told me with the utmost confidence, "We will have no difficulties raising our child. All he needs is love."

The Art of Grandparenting

The next day my son and I took a bus to Safed to buy thirty-six diapers and a bucket to wash them in. We also stopped at the townhall to register the newborn citizen, since his parents had missed the opportunity to do so when storming out of the maternity ward. It is customary in Judaism to keep the name of a boy more or less secret until the moment of the circumcision, which takes place on the eighth day. I had been present when my son and his wife discussed possible names. Although I believed they had opted for the name Noach, which in Hebrew means *comfortable* or *relaxed*, I was not sure of their decision.

Of course, I could not resist stealing a glance on the registration form while my son was filling it out. When I read the name Perre-Adam which means *savage* or *primitive man*, I jumped up, grabbed the form and told the official that he should not accept it, because the mother would never agree to such a crazy name for her baby. My son uttered a few resounding curses and shouted that he would sue the official if he didn't comply. The official banged the identity papers on the counter. My son tore up the form and threw the shreds on the floor. The official ordered the enraged father and his impossible mother out of the building. We sat on a bench in the burning sun. Shaking with anger, my son declared that he didn't need any stupid forms to call his son whatever he wanted. After a while, however, he handed me his identity papers. I returned to the almighty official and begged him to forgive an excited child-father, pity a mother who didn't know Hebrew, and keep in mind the future of an innocent baby. I received a new form and registered my grandson as Noach. Although I was convinced I had acted in the child's best interest, this is one of the stories I don't like to tell.

But of course, a grandmother is not her grandchildren's only source of information. As a teenager Noach accused me of having prevented him from bearing the unique name his father had chosen for him.

THE ART OF GRANDPARENTING

I believe he has forgiven me, for I see him often and we are close friends. Nevertheless, when his own daughter was born, two years ago, he gave her a name that is every bit as controversial as the one he himself had missed.

A beautiful story of which my grandchildren know only the beginning and the end, concerns the one child (out of eight) who came to us as a special present from the powers that be. Although Shai entered our family when he was four, we had to wait three years before we could legally adopt him. On that day we were so happy that we allowed all our children to play truant from school. Seeing a family of ten entering the courtroom, the bewildered judge asked, "What's this? Who are you going to adopt?" Before my husband or I could say a word, seven-year-old Shai stepped forward and announced in a clear voice: "All of them, Mister Judge. I am adopting the whole family." After that there was no more need to mention the adoption. Till this very day, if a busybody asks, "Who of your children is the adopted one?" my husband and I always answer, "We don't remember."

Nevertheless, when Shai, at twenty-eight, sensed that something more than simple friendship was growing between him and Josephina, he told her right away, "Before we continue our relationship, I want you to know that I am adopted." A year after they were married they presented us with our sixteenth grandchild. When Haleli was four, I thought it wise to drop an occasional hint that would prepare her for the day she would learn about her father's origins. Thus I would sometimes take out the family album and nonchalantly mention, "Unfortunately I have no pictures of Shai as a baby, since he was not yet our son at that time." Or I would say about a certain event, "This happened before Shai became a member of our family." The reward for my discretion was a rap over the knuckles from Josephina who strictly forbade me to hint at Shai's adoption in the presence of their daughter. "The situation is much too complex for a layman to handle it," she told me unambiguously. "Don't you ever again make the slightest allusion to Shai's past."

Meanwhile I had written a book about the Israeli experience during its first fifty years, and many of my characters were based on existing people. True, I had changed all the names, but anybody who wanted to find out who was who, could easily do so. Before I had sent out my manuscript, I had asked all the members of our family if they agreed to figure in my book. Shai had been the first to give his OK. "And since we are at it," he had added, "why did you change my name? What are you afraid of?"

His daughter could not read yet, but I didn't doubt that sooner or later people would talk. Three months before the book was due to appear, I said to Shai, "Either you tell Haleli that you are adopted, or I do it." Shai said nothing.

Two weeks after this one-way conversation my husband turned eighty. During the party I showed our guests an ancient ten-minute movie in which our children had acted the story of Moses in the bulrushes. The climax of the story is of course when Faro's daughter lifts the baby out of his floating basket and calls out, "The God of the Hebrews has given me a son!" This was the moment that four-year-old Haleli chose to exclaim in the pitch-dark room full of visitors, "Grandma, do you remember how once upon a time my daddy came out of a different mother, and how happy you were when she allowed you to have him?"

I never tell about my fight with Josefina, but the part about Moses in the bulrushes has become Haleli's favored story.

Each time I tell it to her, she adds, "When my dad was adopted, he did not only get a father and a mother, but he also got all these brothers and sisters who afterwards became my uncles and aunts."

THE ART OF GRANDPARENTING

Then we hug each other and she adds, "In this way my daddy's luck became also my luck."

And I answer, "And mine! Not every grandmother is blessed with a wonderful granddaughter like you."

Experienced as I may be, there is not a grandchild who has not at one time or another confronted me with the unexpected. When our youngest daughter had her third child in France, I flew over to take care of Bert, aged ten and Yon, aged five. One beautiful winter's day, when I had to accompany Bert to his guitar lesson, I took Yon along. I promised him we would play in the freshly fallen snow during the half hour we had to wait for his brother. Initially he seemed happy enough, but the moment Bert disappeared inside the teacher's house, Yon threw a tantrum, such as I had never witnessed in my long carreer of mother and grandmother. He threw himself on the ground and screamed that I should fetch his brother immediately. If not, he had no desire to live any longer and would stab himself to death with his mother's carving knife as soon as we came home. Since I had no intention of letting my own grandson blackmail me, the only thing I could do was waiting the full half hour until the lesson was over and Bert would emerge from the building. In the meantime Yon continued to roll in the snow and hurt himself with sticks and stones he picked up from the ground. He became so wet that I genuinely feared he might catch pneumonia. He cried with cold and misery, but kicked me viciously at every attempt I made to pick him up. Even after his brother had joined us and the three of us undertook the jouney home, Yon continued to scream and threaten he would kill himself with the carving knife this very evening.

When we came home he ran upstairs, told his mother how badly I had treated him, and allowed her to rub him dry and change his clothes. After this he came downstairs and played with his toy cars. As for me, I tried to minimize the event so as not to upset my daughter, but I kept a close watch over my grandson each time he left the living room. I worried so much that I secretly locked the kitchen for the night. In fact the fright has not left me till this very day.

Came Shabbat eve, which is a festive occasion in most Jewish families, even those who don't define themselves as religious. One thing my daughter likes to do on Friday after dinner is asking all people present what has been their most beautiful experience during the week. In general, there are many different answers. But this time the birth of a new son, brother and grandson took first place for everybody except Yon, who firmly insisted that his best experience had been a hike in the snow with his grandmother.

"But Yon," I couldn't resist commenting, "you wanted to kill yourself after that hike."

"Come on, grandma" said my five-year-old grandson, "that is the way people express themselves nowadays. Don't you ever watch television?"

Although I love the ending, this story falls into the category: Don't tell.

A story which also falls into the same category involves a granddaughter who lives in Holland and, perhaps because of this, is more attached to the Jewish religion than her Israeli cousins. Fortunately, she is bilingual, so we have no difficulties communicating whenever she visits, which is almost every summer.

When Rose was fourteen she decided to accompany her mother and me to the liberal synagogue in Jerusalem where we are members. The occasion was *Tisha beAv*, the day that Jews all over the world commemorate the destruction of the temple which has resulted in

THE ART OF GRANDPARENTING

a diaspora of two thousand years. When we were about to leave the house, I saw that Rose was wearing a miniskirt and a shirt with a conspicuously low neckline.

"Darling," I said, "may I please ask you to dress more appropriately? Remember we are going to the synagogue and this is a day of mourning."

These simple words provoked a tsunami of tears. To repeat the contents of my granddaughter's diatribe would be impossible, but in between cries and hickups she managed to convey that nobody appreciated her, nobody understood her, nobody loved her, and that she would never change her dress simply because her grandmother's notions were as old-fashioned as those of a dinosauer.

Angrily I told her that I would be ashamed to appear in our synagogue, liberal as it may be, with a granddaughter dressed up like a streetwalker. With this I slammed the door and marched away accompanied by my crestfallen daughter.

"Why did you antagonize Rosy?" she whimpered. "She is only a child, and I so much wanted her to come to the service."

"Does she dress like this when she goes to a service in Amsterdam?" I asked.

"Of course not, but our synagogue is more orthodox."

"Aha," I answered tartly. "In Amsterdam, no and in Jerusalem, yes? Well, it won't happen. I'll see to that." We walked on in an uneasy silence. But when we arrived at the synagogue, who was waiting for us at the gate if not Rose, decently dressed and mightily pleased because her grandfather had shown her a shortcut that we, the old cronies, didn't know.

Unfortunately not every confrontation is solved so easily. At least one fight with a grandchild caused me much heartbreak and a

The Art of Grandparenting

sleepless night. It happened on one of those happy days that ten or twelve of our grandchildren were playing a party game around the table. A row broke out when a younger child tried to cheat on an older cousin. Maybe I should not have intervened, or else I should have realized that Daniel at fifteen was still as eager to win as his younger siblings and cousins. Instead, I uttered some platitude to the extent that the oldest should be the wisest. Towering over me with head and shoulders, and with tears in his eyes, Daniel shouted at me, "If that's how it is, I am leaving."

Stupidly I made my second serious mistake within two minutes. "Very well," I shouted back. "Good riddance and don't come back."

Overturning his chair and slamming the door Daniel tore out of the room. The others resumed their game. Peace was restored. It was only towards evening, when Daniel had not returned home, that I realized that I had actually banned my own grandson from our house.

I spent the night and the following day torturing myself with visions of traffic accidents, drugs, seduction, abduction and murder. Fortunately non of these catastrophees happened. After having bivouacked in a parking place and spent the day roaming in the old city of Jerusalem, Daniel showed up at a neighbor who, like Noach's dove, was sent forth to explore the situation. In short, all was well that ended well, but I had learned my lesson. There is a great difference between telling a prissy girl that you don't want to see her in synagogue if she is not properly dressed (since this is the exact truth), and telling an agrieved teenager that he doesn't have to come home (since this is as far from the truth as ever can be).

Only last month I made another grave mistake. It was in connection with the Seder night when families gather at a festive meal and reminisce about the Biblical Exodus. According to Judaism, it is the duty of the older generation to transmit to their offspring that once upon a time we were slaves in Egypt, and that now we are free people living in our own land. Since this opens the door for all kind of philosophical and political reflections concerning our behavior in the present time, my husband and I are specially keen on celebrating the Seder night with as many grandchildren as possible.

Of course, we accept the fact that our married children celebrate alternately with us and with their inlaws. This year, however, I was cheated out of my turn by the children of our son Yannay, whose wife left him eight years ago. Although I had invited the children a month in advance, reminding them several times that last year they had been with their mother, I heard only at the very last minute that they, as well as their father, would celebrate with the other family.

Although we had a house full of grandchildren and a wonderful Seder, I felt heavily let down. Why had Yannay's children done this to me and why had they not told me about their decision at an earlier stage? It took me a few days to realize that I had myself to blame.

Although the divorce has caused Yannay a great deal of sorrow, he has maintained a correct relationship with his former wife, thereby consciously disregarding his own feelings to spare those of his children. Obviously, the children had waited till the very last moment to see if I would invite their mother, too. When they realized that no invitation was forthcoming, while their father is always welcome at the home of his former in-laws, they chose to celebrate with father and mother even though they are no longer a real family. So what is the conclusion? If I want Yannay's children to celebrate the Seder with us, I must invite their mother too. This is what I am going to do next year.

In which catagory, tell or don't tell, this story will eventually fall depends on the outcome.

the Art of Grandparenting

Tips & Tricks

It is best to let the young parents name their own children, even if you feel their choice is ill-advised and this makes you want to speak out of turn.

If there is a family secret, it may best be revealed through a story. If the story is Biblical, so much the better. The listener will draw their own conclusions.

Grandchildren will bring you the unexpected. When they do, remember the adage: *All's well that ends well.*

Teenagers will test your resolve. They may wear outlandish clothes, and when you object, they may try to get their way. Stand firm. That's really what they want you to do.

If divorce enters the family, for the sake of the children, always welcome the parent who is no longer part of your family into your home. It is best for everyone.

Surprises, Traditions and the Teacher in Us All

Judith Mammay

SITTING DOWN TO WRITE THIS LETTER to all you new grandparents, I planned to talk about how to deal with the surprises that our grandchildren sometimes present to us. However, once I started to write, other points came to mind. The first of these is the establishment of traditions. Another, since I am a teacher, is how even the simplest interactions with our grandchildren reveal our role as teachers. With these three ideas firmly in mind—surprises, traditions, and grandparents as teachers—I will continue with my story.

As children we usually develop some sort of relationship with our own grandparents. Then we grow up, have our own kids, and help them develop relationships with their grandparents —our parents and in-laws. Then our kids grow up and move out of our house. Time passes and we look forward to meeting our own grandchildren, sometimes much to the chagrin of our children who tell us they aren't ready for a family. We imagine our own relationships with our grandchildren, basing these on our own past experiences.

I grew up outside a small New England town where my great-grandmother and great-aunt, my grandfather and grandmother,

THE ART OF GRANDPARENTING

three aunts and uncles, and three cousins lived within a quarter mile of my own family of five. At a young age I was able to walk or ride my bike throughout the neighborhood to any of their houses, at any given time, unaccompanied—remember, it was very different back then; kids had more freedom because there was less crime.

I enjoyed visiting my great-grandmother, great-aunt and my grandparents often. My great-grandmother was in her nineties by the time I was able to go there by myself, and I remember her sitting and knitting. She walked slowly with her 'horses' as she called them, four-legged crutch-type supports with a box in the middle to transport whatever she needed. She used these because earlier in life she had injured her leg in a fall and it had not healed properly.

I have many fond memories about my grandfather mostly because he had a large garden and kept chickens. My cousins and I were always welcome to hold the baby chicks every spring and to feed the hens and gather eggs year-round. We also helped in the garden, picking strawberries, peas, and beans, among other things. "Tomorrow is a pickin' day," Grandpa would say. "Be here early." Then, when we were ready to pick, he'd warn us, "Don't eat TOO many!" Grandpa also gave us directions for plucking the chickens, certainly different from just picking up a packaged chicken at the grocery. I was mesmerized as he grabbed a chicken from the coop, brought it to the chopping block, and then with little fanfare chopped its head off with the axe. He released it to the yard, where it flopped around like crazy for a short time while Grandpa repeated the process with three or four more chickens. He then strung them up to drain. It all seemed natural, just something you have to do if you want to eat a chicken for dinner.

He had a couple of sawhorses set up in the yard with an old wooden door across them for us to use as a table. "Spread out the newspapers," he said. When we had done that, he dipped each chicken in turn into the boiling water and then set one in front of each of us. "Do it this way," he would say as he showed us how to pull the feathers against the direction they grew for best results. "And make sure you get all the pinfeathers."

What I remember most, though, were my family's time-honored traditions. We had a rule that we still honor today as much as possible: "Kids belong at home on Christmas morning." For that reason, we always planned our large family gathering to celebrate Christmas on Christmas Eve. At first, we gathered at my great-grandmother's house, but as she grew older, we shifted the celebrations to my grandparents' house. Scalloped oysters topped the menu, the kids always sat at their own table, and after the meal, kids always helped with the dishes. No one used paper plates at a formal meal back in those days. Then all the grandchildren stood up and sang Christmas carols before we passed out the huge stack of gifts under the tree.

Each summer a similar family get-together occurred in Grandpa's back yard on the weekend closest to August 16th. Maybe this date won favor because the town celebrated "Bennington Battle Day" on that weekend, or perhaps because August 16th was my out-of-state aunt's birthday. It might have been because by that time in the summer the sweet corn was ready for harvesting from Grandpa's garden. Along with the fresh corn, we steamed clams, grilled chicken on the grate of my grandfather's outdoor brick fireplace, and consumed numerous salads, home made baked beans, and desserts we all contributed to the feast.

Thanksgiving ranked as our third traditional celebration each year as we gathered at Grandpa and Grandma's house, everyone arriving with sumptuous platters, casseroles and desserts to contribute to the holiday.

As my siblings and I grew up, we eventually moved away, and in time we created our own families, making it harder to maintain all

The Art of Grandparenting

of these traditions as a family. But we tried. Keeping to the 'home on Christmas' rule, we moved our family celebrations to the weekend before Christmas. With the passing of the two older generations, my parents' home became our holiday destination for the weekend so we could keep the tradition alive and well.

My husband and I keep both the 'rule' and the Christmas tradition going with our own boys and their families, but this is not always easy. One year we celebrated Thanksgiving on Thursday and Christmas only two days later, because two of our sons were in the military—one headed to Korea and the other to be stationed in Germany that year.

More recently, two of our three boys live close by, making holidays easier to celebrate. Our grandchildren now come to our home, bringing with them all the boisterous excitement of the season. We still serve up our traditional meal, although hot chicken salad and chili —both from old family recipes— replace the scalloped oysters. And we never know how the little ones will delight us.

One year, my son dropped off our then three-year-old grandson early (so Santa and his helpers could assemble a swing set in his back yard). As a diversion, I figured he'd have a great time making sugar cookies. We mixed the dough, rolled it out, cut the shapes, baked them, and then frosted and decorated them. Everyone made a big deal of the cookies as we passed them around the table for dessert later that evening, but when the plate came to my grandson, he would have nothing to do with the cookies.

"No, thank you," he said. "I want REAL cookies." After the laughter subsided, I granted his request by opening up our cookie drawer and pulling out the store-bought cookies just for him.

My advice to new grandparents: carry on traditions from your past as much as possible. If you come from a family that had no traditions or had ones that cannot be preserved, create your own new traditions. If you have the luxury of living close to your grandkids, it will be easy. If you don't, you'll need to be more creative.

If health, distance, or money keep you from being with your grandchildren frequently, perhaps it would be good to establish a special time each week to call and talk with them. A letter in the mail each week or once a month could be something they would come to look forward to. With our far-away grandsons, we had their parents set up email accounts for the boys and we emailed them. We did not often get a response, but at least they heard from us.

Regular summer visits, either at their homes or yours without parents is another alternative. We usually have our son and his family here for a week or so in June or July, and we have the kids for a few days while the parents take some time for themselves. We always try to take one or two special trips to a museum or water park, but also plan less organized activities like going to the beach or the pool, taking bike rides around our park, or just hanging out.

Meeting at a lake or the beach, or at a mountain retreat for a week during the summer could also be an option, especially if there is a family summer home. When our kids were growing up, we liked to camp, and sometime my parents joined us. One summer we rented a cabin for a week on a lake in northern New Hampshire about an equal distance from our house, my brother's house, and my parents' house, and we all met there. The possibilities are endless, and it does not make a difference if it is something grand or small, as long as it becomes a tradition and a regular time to spend time with you so your grandchildren can look forward to as kids and look back on as they grow into adults, one day to have their own kids.

As grandparents, we have the unique opportunity to shape our grandkids' lives and attitudes in small ways. One thing we need

THE ART OF GRANDPARENTING

to remember is that the phrase *'do as I say and not as I do'* does not work. Kids are great observers and are really good at mimicking, so be prepared to see and hear yourself in them. As role models, we need to be careful of what we say and how we act in front of our grandchildren, if we don't want to see them repeating what they see and hear.

I am a teacher by profession, so much so that it can be easily recognized by others. One day I was checking out at a store and struck up a conversation with the sales clerk. The stranger behind me said, "You're a teacher, aren't you?" I'm not sure what I said or did to elicit the comment, but my point is that we grandparents do not have to be professional teachers to influence our grandchildren. In fact, if the kids think we are trying to teach them something they might rebel by being unwilling to join in the activity we have planned or to listen to any commentary from us at that particular moment. So rather than setting about to teach, we are better advised to provide them with opportunities to simply expand their horizons. They'll take away what they want to keep.

I am fortunate that some of my grandchildren visit me weekly. One of my favorite activities with them is to visit the library, starting when they are two years old. My days together with the oldest local grandchild never coordinated with the weekly preschool story-time, so we set up our own private story time to read the four or five books he chose at the library. Other times he chose play with the puzzles and toys or use the computer. But we lugged home a bag full of books to read between library visits. Now that he is older, he is more independent during our visits and reads to himself. He sends me off to gather the books we will check out. "You pick out the books," he says. "I like the books you pick out better."

The library is also a good place to visit even when the grandkids come only once or twice a year. I take my two far-away grandsons to the library on the first day of their week-long visits.

The Art of Grandparenting

Another favorite activity is 'exploring' in the woods. Sometimes we walk in the forest at the end of the street; on other occasions we will drive to one of the many parks in the area that has walking trails. For fun, I give them either binoculars or a digital camera to take photos of interesting things they find. This helps them to focus on the beauty of nature and gives us a chance to discuss some of the different types of birds, bugs, and plants we see along the way. At home we can download the pictures to see what treasures we captured. Who knows—maybe they are developing a life-long love of nature and the outdoors. Maybe they will develop a hobby or even a career that involves photography.

Often, the kids enjoy just helping around the house. Grinding nuts, squeezing lemons, washing potatoes, setting the table, and baking cookies are among my grandchildren's favorite activities.

The important thing is to be observant. Watch for what might interest your grandkids and then choose age-and-interest appropriate outings and activities.

Young kids have shorter attention spans and may want to quit in the middle of longer projects such as baking cookies. Let them go, but to increase a child's attention span, it is a good idea to negotiate with them a little bit, encouraging them to work for two more minutes or to decorate three more cookies. Over time, this can encourage them to stick with activities even after they lose interest.

Having fun is the most important thing of all. Sometimes just following the kids' leads may teach us a thing or two. One day my five-year-old grandson announced on the way home from school that we were going to do a project.

"It's not hard," he said. "We just need scissors and crayons and paper."

"Okay," I answered. "What are we going to make?"

"First we are going to make a rainbow, and then we are going to make a fogbow."

The Art of Grandparenting

"What's a fogbow?" I asked.

"It's a white rainbow."

Not one to question the imagination of a child, I agreed, and we did indeed make both rainbows and fogbows. About the time we were finishing, my husband came into the room.

"What are you making?" Papa asked.

My grandson held up his creations. "This is a rainbow, and this is a fogbow," he answered.

"There's no such thing as a fogbow," said Papa.

"Yes, there is."

"I don't think so," Papa said, heading for his computer, where he Googled 'fogbows.' A couple minutes later he was back.

"I apologize," Papa said. "You are right—there ARE fogbows."

"I knew that," said my grandson. "I read about them in my *100 Things You Should Know about the Weather* book," which we had given him the previous Christmas.

Occasionally, parents and grandparents will receive a 'surprise' with the birth of a child. We want to think of babies as being born healthy and cute, but if there are some who are not, they certainly will not belong to us. However, this is not always the case. Sometimes our grandchildren are born with birth defects. Sometimes problems are not always obvious at birth, but become obvious later. Some of these are genetic disabilities and some can be caused by birth injuries. These include Down syndrome, cerebral palsy, spina bifida, and autism, among others. I do not know the statistics for most, but for autism, recent statistics show that as many as one child out of every 150 has some level of autism.

If a grandchild has a disability, parents and grandparents may initially be shocked and go through a grieving period. This is normal,

THE ART OF GRANDPARENTING

but then it is time to move on. Grandparents can help considerably in the process through a number of ways. Most importantly, support the parents in any way you can. Be there for them. Research the disability and understand as much as you can to put the whole situation into perspective. Take things day by day.

This happened to me. My first two grandsons were born in Germany during the three years my son was stationed there. We visited just after the first was born, then didn't see them again until they returned home three years later.

When I met the younger one, I noticed he was not doing what most one-year-old kids do. Instead of crawling around getting into everything, he sat where he was placed and stayed there. He also did not babble like most kids. He was either silent or screaming. I knew almost immediately what the problem was. However, my son and his wife were aware that my grandson was falling behind developmentally and were already consulting with doctors and seeking speech evaluations. So I said nothing.

I felt fortunate because I had changed my teaching emphasis to special education, and in my training I learned about the disabilities afflicting my young students. I felt I could be a resource for my son's family when the time came.

It was several months and many doctor visits later that my daughter-in-law finally asked me, "What do you think it is?"

Without telling her my suspicions, I went to my computer, printed out a list of signs and symptoms, and handed it to her. As she read the list, she ticked off each item—"Yes, yes, yes, yes, yes...." This simple list helped her to identify that my grandson had autism.

Autism, unlike some other disabilities, is not readily recognized at birth. A friend, Bette, who has a granddaughter with autism, shared her story with me.

Bette and her husband lived about four hours away from her son and his family so did not see them very often. During one visit, she and her husband, both experienced educators, recognized that their two-year-old granddaughter seemed developmentally off track. They tried to share their concerns about their granddaughter's lack of development, pointing out the significant differences between her and her older sister at the same age. The parents became so upset and defensive that they packed up and left at eight o'clock at night in spite of the long, four-hour drive home.

Bette's daughter-in-law refused to talk with them and her son spoke very little with them over the next year. Finally they began to realize and accept that their daughter was falling behind. Then they apologized to Bette and asked for help.

A grandchild with special needs can cause much stress in extended family relationships in a variety of ways. But special kids can also bring a great deal of joy into the family if given a chance. My grandson frequently makes me laugh with the things he says and his perspective of the world. One day his parents were discussing their babysitter, who was pregnant, and my grandson said, "She has an embryo." A few weeks later, at just the right time, he announced, "She now has a fetus."

The rules are the same as for regular kids. Respect your grandchildren and expect respect from them. Talk with them, listen to them, play with them and accept them for who they are no matter what their developmental level.

As a grandparent you are in a unique position to share your family traditions and create positive memories for your grandkids. Make a positive difference in the lives of your grandkids. Grow and learn through your experiences with your grandchildren. Take good advantage of the awe-inspiring opportunity that has come to you — to be a grandparent.

The Art of Grandparenting

Tips & Tricks

Take your grandkids to the library.

Take your grandkids exploring in the woods.

Engage your grandkids in helping around the house.

Do projects the grandkids think up on their own; you might learn something new!

Keep in touch by phone, letters, or email, or all three!

Adjust your holiday get-togethers to fit changing schedules. The holidays can be celebrated weeks before or after the real date.

If your grandchild has special needs, most importantly, support the parents in any way you can. Be there for them.

Research the disability and understand as much as you can to put the whole situation into perspective.

Take things day by day.

Remember, you have already raised your family. It's great to help out with babysitting, etc. but know your limits and set your boundaries early.

Spend individual time with each of your grandchildren, but don't show favorites. Kids are quick to pick up on that.

Avoid the 'present' trap. Save gifts for special occasions rather than overdoing it. Give the gift of your time and involvement. It's better for kids to look forward to your visits rather than to the gifts you bring them.

To Grandparents-in-Waiting

Rochelle Jewel Shapiro

Of all the things I wasn't expecting when I had a granddaughter it was that she wouldn't like me.

I knew just how it began. I was proud that my daughter, Heather, was nursing Rebecca as I had her. I enjoyed my granddaughter's snorty sounds as she fed and I loved when her tiny dimpled hand rose to pat my daughter's breast. But there wasn't much time to bond with her. I was only handed the baby when Heather and her husband, Jesse, went out. Putting the baby to bed was stressful to them. They had devised an elaborate and rigid bedtime ritual and didn't want any deviation from it. The two of them were so sleep-deprived and frazzled that it was hard to say anything to them without getting into a big fight. They were in terror over whether or not she would sleep.

I remembered how it felt to be a new mother and want to do everything perfectly. When Heather was an infant I was so worried when she cried that I carried her on me in a snugglee even when I vacuumed the apartment.

"Put her down," my mother-in-law used to say on every visit. "You have to learn to let her cry sometimes or you'll wear yourself out."

THE ART OF GRANDPARENTING

Maybe my mother-in-law was right, but I not only didn't listen to her, with my hormones surging, I hotly resented her for saying it. Worse, when she babysat and I left breast milk in bottles for a feeding, my mother-in-law bought Heather formula instead.

"I wasn't sure your milk was fresh," she'd told me.

I felt like banishing her from our house forever.

From that time on, I resolved that new parents' wishes should be obeyed, like it or not.

"Promise me you'll put Rebecca to bed the way I want," Heather said. She had tacked a manifesto of *Don'ts* on the fridge:

1. Don't feed Rebecca right before bedtime or she'll fall asleep with milk in her mouth and that will jeopardize her budding teeth. Feed her at 5:45pm in her room with only the nightlight on so her eyes get used to the darkness. Then wait until 6:00 to change her and begin putting her to sleep.
2. Don't sing to Rebecca. You'll keep her up. Just put on the white noise machine.
3. Don't rock her in the rocking chair to get her to sleep. We found that she does better if you walk with her, patting her on the back. If she cries, switch her from your left shoulder to your right, still keeping her upright.
4. Don't let her cry. Keep walking with her in her room until she falls asleep and then put her down, but not on her stomach.
5. Don't walk with her outside her bedroom. Stay in her room until she falls asleep because we want her to get the idea that her bedroom is for sleeping.

"I promise," I told Heather.

Routinely, it took between one to two hours for Rebecca to fall asleep. My back ached so that I couldn't stand it. It felt claustrophobic in the dark room and the rainy sound of the white noise machine made me have to pee.

When Heather and Jesse came to visit us, I thought it would be more relaxed in my own environment. But even though Rebecca slept in her own room at their house in Upstate N.Y., Heather and Jesse didn't want her to sleep in our other spare bedroom where they were afraid they wouldn't hear her cry. With the pull-out bed and her crib in our guest room, I only had a narrow lane to walk in. As I paced the darkness with her, I'd stub my toe on the metal base of the trundle bed.

This routine made what should have been pleasurable, holding my granddaughter in my arms, excruciating, like water boarding. When she finally fell asleep, I heaved a sigh of relief and gingerly put her down in her crib. I tiptoed out and then I heard her wail and I had to pick her up again.

I felt trapped, then rebellious like a teenager. If I could only sit down in a chair and rock her in my arms, I thought. Who would know the difference? But then I worried that Heather would somehow sneak up and catch me as she had when I tried to put money under her pillow from the Tooth Fairy. Suddenly, the bright beam of a flashlight swung into my face.

"Gotcha," she'd said.

No, I'd hear Heather if she came home, I thought. The key would turn in the lock. I could go out to the living room and watch TV as I put Rebecca to sleep. Then a crazy thought came to me. What if they had hidden video cameras running, the kind people have to trap a nanny? Maybe if I sat down in a dark room, they couldn't see me. Weren't there video cameras that took clear pictures in the dark? But you'd have to be in the military to get your hands on them, wouldn't you? On Ebay, you could buy anything.

The Art of Grandparenting

After awhile, I was beyond caring who caught me. I carried Rebecca into the living room where my husband, Bernie, sat in his recliner watching *Law & Order*. He worked thirteen hours a day in his pharmacy with a forty minute commute each way without traffic or bad weather, and that hadn't changed when he became a grandfather. Since I worked from home as a writer, even though I worked long hours, I was practically retired compared to him. I ended up doing all the childcare so he could watch TV for a half hour before he went to bed.

"Bernie," I said, "Rebecca won't fall asleep. I can't keep pacing in the dark anymore."

His brows rose up over the gold frames of his glasses in surprise. "Let me try," he said, and got up from his squeaky recliner.

"Make sure you read the list on the fridge so that you don't violate the rules," I told him.

With Rebecca in his arms, I watched him read the list, nodding as he went down. I settled into the recliner that had been pre-warmed by his 6'4" body.

After an hour, I got up and peeked into the guest room to see how he was doing. With the aid of the hallway light, I saw that Rebecca was already asleep against him, her pudgy cheek squished against his shoulder, but Bernie still paced with her, a look of ecstasy on his face as he cocked his head towards hers. He was making up for what he had missed when our children were young.

The only real time we had with Rebecca was putting her to sleep. Jesse and Heather were too nervous to let us take her anywhere in our car and there were no sidewalks in their neighborhood to take her out for a walk in a stroller. In our neighborhood they were unsettled by the cars speeding through intersections and didn't want us to take her out by ourselves there either. In fact, unless it was bedtime, they were reluctant to leave us alone with her.

THE ART OF GRANDPARENTING

When Rebecca approached two, I was walking up her driveway next to Bernie as we arrived for one of our visits.

"Grandpa, grandpa," she shouted out the window, ignoring me.

"Say hello to Grandma," Bernie said when we came in.

"Hello," she said without making eye contact. "Grandpa, Grandpa, up, up," she cried out.

"Look what I brought you, Rebecca," I said, taking a wooden puzzle out of a bag.

She took it from me. "Grandpa, come to my room," she said. She grabbed his hand, and led him to her room, closing the door behind her.

I let it go. But on our next visit, when I held my arms out to her, she turned away.

"Grandpa, Grandpa, I want Grandpa," she insisted.

My husband looked so miserable to be preferred over me. "Let's all play Ring Around A-Rosie," he suggested.

When I tried to join hands, Rebecca shouted, "No Grandma, just Grandpa."

"Say you're sorry to Grandma," Heather said. "You hurt her feelings."

"No," Rebecca said, face flushed, tears trembling in her brown eyes.

Heather was ready to give her a time out.

"Don't force her," I whispered. "She'll come to care for me in time."

And time passed, a whole year, but she still rebuffed me.

When my daughter phoned, I said, "Please don't ask Rebecca if she'd like to speak to me until she asks to herself." I just couldn't bear to hear her say again, "No, I only want to talk to Grandpa."

On our monthly, sometimes bi-monthly visits, Rebecca would say, "I love you, Grandpa," and give me her tiny cold shoulder.

I knew that children sometimes rejected one parent in favor of the other for a time, but Rebecca's rejection of me was extreme, blatant. It hit me so hard that I began to do things I hadn't done since

THE ART OF GRANDPARENTING

I was a teenager: sniff at my armpits to check if my deodorant worked, cup my hands over my mouth and nose and exhale to see if my breath smelled, examine my face closely in the mirror for blemishes.

A whole year ensued of "No Grandma's, only Grandpa."

"I had no idea that when I took over bedtime it would lead to this," Bernie said. "I should have told Heather that her mother needed to sit in a chair if she were going to hold Rebecca for long periods of time."

"At least I didn't lose my relationship with Heather and Jesse," I said. "But I am afraid I've lost my 'in' with Rebecca."

"She'll come to love you," he said, and kissed me.

As usual, when I tried to read a book to her, she snatched it from my hands and gave it to Bernie. "Read to me, Grandpa."

The next visit I by-passed the book and told her the story of *Goldilocks and the Three Bears*. I could tell she was listening, but she didn't make eye contact with me or comment in any way. Over the next two visits, even though she didn't ask me to tell her fairy tales, I continued to tell them with the same result.

On the following visit (she was three and a half then,) I told her the story of when her mother was just her age and brought a gerbil home from the science room at school to care for over a holiday. Rebecca looked directly at me. Encouraged, I drew a gerbil for her and went on:

"Mommy managed to take the gerbil out of the cage and put a tiny doll dress on it. And then…oh, oh..(said with open mouth and hands to cheeks) the gerbil got away. We searched and searched, but couldn't find it anywhere." (Rebecca's mouth was open and her hands were on her cheeks too.) And then, we heard the woman next door scream, 'Eek, a mouse wearing a dress,' and Mommy and I knew just what to do. We got out the butterfly net and some gerbil food." (I drew a picture of a butterfly net for Rebecca.) "Then we rang the

The Art of Grandparenting

neighbor's doorbell and put gerbil food in the corner and waited. When the gerbil came for it, what do you think we did? We captured him in the butterfly net. "

Rebecca almost fell off her chair laughing.

"Another story, Grandma," she said.

With my heart beating wildly, I began: "Once upon a time, in cold winter, your mother was outside with Uncle Charles. Uncle Charles loved to climb trees back then. He climbed to the highest limb, but this time, he couldn't get down. Mommy grew tired of waiting for him to come down, so she came in out of the cold.

"Soon Charles began to shout for help. 'Eek, eek,' he cried out.

"The upstairs neighbor, Mr. Gussack, the mayor of our town, looked out his window. He thought he saw a giant bluebird with a strange cry. But then he looked closer and saw it was your Uncle Charles wearing a blue snowsuit.

"'What are you doing up in that tree?' Mr. Gussack asked.

'I'm stuck,' Charles said, his breath making little eeks in the air."

Rebecca's leaned closer to me, wide-eyed.

"Mr. Gussack called me on the phone," I continued. "'Charles is stuck up in a tree,' he said.

"I called the fire department. 'Wah, wah, wah,' the engines wailed. Pretty soon the firemen put a ladder up to the tall tree. One climbed up and helped Charles down the ladder.

"'Why didn't you tell me Charles was stuck in a tall tree?' I asked your mommy when we were all inside, safe and warm.

"Your mommy shrugged her shoulders. (I shrugged mine.) 'I forgot,' she said."

Rebecca hugged me hard. "Tell me another, Grandma."

I was giddy. Like Scheherazade, I had wooed her with stories.

After that my husband was a happier grandpa, too. He no longer had to feel guilty that I was shunned while he was fawned

THE ART OF GRANDPARENTING

over. In fact, she began to greet me first "Story, Grandma, story," she demanded, bouncing on her toes, clapping.

To play fair, on subsequent visits I had to go on outings with my daughter so that my husband could have his time alone with Rebecca, too.

Soon the stories I told Rebecca began to take on a pattern that she particularly enjoyed. "Once upon a time there was a little girl named Mommy," was how they would begin. There always managed to be a lot of "eeks" in them as well.

And now, at four, Rebecca calls me on the phone everyday to ask for stories. Her requests usually sound like this:

"Tell me about when Mommy was a little girl and she was outside with Uncle Charles and Uncle Charles climbed a tall tree and got stuck in the highest branch and couldn't get down and Mommy came inside and didn't tell anyone." (She takes a quick breath.) And Uncle Charles was wearing a blue snowsuit and he called out, 'Eek, eek, eek,'" and the mayor thought he was a bluebird and..."

All I have to do is repeat the story back to her.

The other day, my daughter reported that Rebecca said, "You know, Mommy, I used to only love Grandpa, but now I love Grandma too."

So, grandparents-in-waiting, here is my advice to you. Don't antagonize new parents. Do whatever they say, except if it will cost you a fortune or break your back. And gather your stories like sugarplums to dance in your grandchildren's heads.

the Art of Grandparenting

Tips & Tricks

Try not to antagonize your new-parent children.

Follow the "rules" your new-parent children devise for you, except if it hurts your back or breaks the bank.

When your grandchild favors your spouse over you, put the hurt feelings on hold as you think of ways to find your own path into the grandchild's heart.

Tell stories that are about the grandchild's "Mommy" or "Daddy," starting with: *Once upon a time there was a little girl named Mommy...* OR *Once upon a time there was a little boy named Daddy...*

Draw pictures that illustrate the stories as you go along.

Use funny voices, sounds and gestures to punctuate your real-life made-up stories about the grandchild's parents.

Gather your stories like sugarplums to dance in your grandchildren's heads.

Instant Grandma

Gerri Helms

AT AGE FIFTY, AND SINGLE FOR SEVERAL YEARS, a friend suggested that I write a letter to God and tell Him what I wanted in a man. This seemed like a very odd request for someone as busy as God, but what the heck; my friend had done just that, written a letter to God several years ago, and met the man of her dreams. He lived in the apartment downstairs for over a year, and their paths had never crossed. Five days after writing her letter, they met at the mailbox and well, now you know the rest of that story.

If it worked for her, maybe it would work for me. As a Christian, I'd prayed to God for many unorthodox things. Five years earlier, after a lifetime of morbid obesity, I turned to God instead of the multitude of weight loss schemes of the past. When I took a spiritual approach to weight loss and health, the weight just melted away. It took about a year to lose over one-hundred pounds, and here's the clincher, I've kept it off ever since. That's a definite God-thing. Otherwise, Ayds Candies would have worked in 1967, when I had five pounds to lose instead of more than one-hundred.

The Art of Grandparenting

God helped with my health, so surely He'd want to help me with something as important as a husband, right?

I commenced to writing the list of qualities for my Mr. Wonderful. My friend warned me that it should be as comprehensive as possible. Hmm. So what would I ask God for in a man? After dating a few divorcés, I knew that I wanted a widower. My logic suggested that if a wife would train a husband and have him for life, he'd be a keeper. Better to look for a keeper. I'd been divorced, so that probably weighed into my logic too. I continued to add to the list:

My dream-man would have to like amusement parks.

He would need to be a non-smoker and a non-drinker, or at most take an occasional libation.

He needed to be self-supporting through his own contributions.

Oh, and I'd like him to share my religion too!

No more than five years older than me.

He'd have to like (or at least tolerate) "my" sports – NASCAR and scuba diving.

He could be handsome too, but that wasn't an absolute.

Great sense of humor— very important.

Grown kids who liked me would be nice.

And grandchildren would be a huge bonus!

I had more items on the list, but these were at the top. When I finally finished the letter, I knelt down at the foot of my bed and read the qualities that were important to me. Would God actually be listening? Would he send this perfect fellow my way? I sure hoped so.

Within a week of my prayer, a friend sent me an email with a hug. It requested that I click on this heart in the email and when I did, landed on a website - AOL's LOVE CONNECTION! Mercy! Who would be so desperate as to find a mate on the internet? It looked like an on-line boyfriend grocery store, not for a discerning woman like me. But wait ... what if HE was in there? Should I look? Dare I?

It was the early days of dating websites, accompanied by the big-news horror stories of axe murderers that lured women to secluded places on-line. Curiosity and loneliness finally won out over my drama queen tendencies, and I ventured into the online boyfriend grocery store world for a look at the produce aisle.

To my utter amazement, when I narrowed the search to a twenty-mile radius of my home, widowed, and close to my age, a handsome man popped up. Could it be him? Could it be the man sent from God? I anxiously sent off an email, telling him a little about me, and waited. Later that night, as I turned on my computer, the melodic voice of the AOL guy said, "You've Got Mail!" He wrote! I wrote back. And so it began.

We exchanged emails, phone calls and finally met for coffee. I was smitten by Dave Helms from the get-go. Wow, he swept me off my feet! It was mutual. He pulled his ad from AOL's Love Connection and we dated exclusively. He really seemed too good to be true – he was the answer to my letter to God.

Dave had three children who seemed accepting of me; their mother had passed away suddenly, about eighteen months earlier. And then there were the two grandchildren. I could not have been happier.

Early in our dating, I was eager to prove that I'd be a good prospective grandma. I asked Dave if he thought that we might be permitted to take the kids to Disney World for the day. His look resembled that of a deer in the headlights, but in an effort to impress me, I suppose, he asked his daughter if we could have the kids for a day. She agreed! I was so excited; I could begin to bond with these little ones who would perhaps someday be my grandchildren.

The Art of Grandparenting

The 'other' Grandma, Mrs. Miller, delivered four-year-old Bradley and his eighteen-month old sister, Cassie, that Saturday, about eleven in the morning. It is hard to say who was more thrilled, the kids or me. Excited is not a sufficient word to describe my mood. I was going to experience what it feels like to be a Grandma!

Our first stop would be Denny's for lunch. I buckled Bradley into the back seat and carefully I lifted little Cassie into her car seat. Oh-oh. The aroma of a dirty diaper wafted past my nose. A slight wave of nausea caught me by surprise, but I quickly recovered. It was so much work to get her into that car seat. No worry—I'd just change her at the restaurant, rather than unbuckle her, and go back into the house. The restaurant was just a few minutes away.

We arrived at Denny's, and Cassie began to voice her displeasure with the mess in her diaper. Who could blame her? Grandpa Dave took Bradley to the table, while I pranced off to the rest room, diaper bag and baby in tow. What a thrill to see people smile at me and my future granddaughter. It felt like I was in Fantasyland, and we were not yet on Disney property. Grandma Miller had not included any diaper changing instructions, but how hard could it be? Take the old one off, and whip on the new one, right?

Wrong.

What luck—the handicapped stall was clear, quite roomy, but without a baby-changing table. No worry, we could do this on the floor. Piece of cake! I then learned how quickly babies can roll. Cassie, intent on escape, performed a quick flip-and-dodge maneuver. Recognizing me as a ringer—inexperienced as a greenhorn on the first cattledrive—she was prepared to win the diaper changing game! Grandma training 101 was underway! One for Cassie, none for Grandma Gerri.

Finally, she settled down on her back, and I attempted to disrobe her lower torso. The bathroom was warm, and the aroma of

THE ART OF GRANDPARENTING

baby poopie ripened like compost in late August. I must have been getting used to it, since the next wave of nausea passed like a breeze in the morning air, and I set about the business of removing the britches from the squiggly baby. Sure, we had a few setbacks, but I still felt confident—after all, I could control a eighteen-month-old baby. *She* was not going to call the shots. *I was.* Right?

Taking charge and firmly grasping the waistband of her pants, my fingers encountered something warm and squishy. Baby poopie! It had oozed up from the back of her diaper, and was not only on her britches but also on her shirt, her legs, her socks, and shoes—and now also on my fingers. Ew, ew, ew! Another wave of nausea. It was overwhelming, but I managed to fight it off and not to throw up on my would-be granddaughter. How was I going to get those pants off? The poop was everywhere.

I tugged again, and managed to wrestle the pants to the floor. Then the diaper. Wow, the smell was more like bio-hazard than human waste! I tried breathing through my mouth, but that was worse. My eyes were watering as I pushed through the urge to purge.

Babies sure do have a lot of creases! Every one of Cassie's was full of poop. How could a two-year-old child produce that much poop? I don't think even I ever pooped that much at one time, and I was nearly fifty years her senior!

We were in desperate need of paper towels. I was wishing that I had grabbed a handful before stretching Cassie out on the floor. Of course, it was next to impossible to keep her in one place. Every time she rolled, poop smeared on the floor, on me, absolutely everywhere. I needed a whole stack of paper towels. I looked up, scanning the bathroom for the towel dispenser, only to discover one of those stupid hand dryers. No paper towels. Not one. There were no tissues in my purse. The toilet paper dispenser was out of reach. I felt my "A" in baby changing quickly slipping away. A lot of good that hand dryer

THE ART OF GRANDPARENTING

machine was going to do me! What did they expect me to do, put the baby in the sink, rinse her off, and then hold her up to blow the water off her butt? Anger, frustration and panic were beginning to set in.

Now what? I ached to get my hands into the sink and wash my poopie fingers. Ah, maybe the diaper bag had a solution to our problems.

Did you ever tell an eighteen-month-old, strange baby, to lay still? They don't know the definition of "lay still while I wash my hands." Now aware that she was in a bathroom with someone she didn't know very well, Cassie started to howl. I mean she emitted blood curdling screams fitting to a Halloween slasher film, the kind a passer-by would hear and instantly suspect a murder in progress. Could this get any worse?

I stood up to wash my hands. No soap. I rinsed my hands the best I could and wiped them on my pants. The squirming baby was looking for escape routes. She could fit nicely under the door. She assumed the belly-flop position and commenced to slither through her escape hatch, without any pants. I grabbed her by the ankles and pulled her back into the stall. She screamed like a banshee!

Reaching into the bag, with one hand, and hanging onto her with the other, I discovered only two disposable diapers and no butt-wiper things either. So, one diaper would be for the baby and the other would have to serve as a wipe. I needed a wet one and a dry one. Did you ever try to tear one of those disposable diapers apart? Not going to happen. They're made of iron! I wondered if Grandma Miller was off smirking somewhere. Was this her demonic plot to demonstrate what a terrible grandma I was going to be? I'd show her, I'd get this kid cleaned up if it was my last act on Earth.

Further one-handed rummaging produced a clean t-shirt. That would have to do as a wash cloth. She wiggled, I wiped. She howled and I begged her to stop. This isn't what I had imagined the day to

THE ART OF GRANDPARENTING

look like. I ran water in the sink and tried to hold her little butt under it. No dice—the sink was too small. The water was now all over the floor, the baby and me. She screamed some more. I was close to screaming too. This grandma stuff was harder than I thought!

After an inordinate amount of time, the poop was finally all off the child and me. She didn't smell too good. I found some baby powder in the bag and generously dumped some on her butt and legs. I also dumped some on my new jeans. They were wet and the powder stuck. It looked like I had done battle with the Pillsbury Dough Boy—and lost. We wrestled some more but I finally got the clean diaper onto her and secured. Miracle!—there was a clean pair of britches, and one more little shirt in the bag. They didn't match, but at this point, I didn't care. Ah, mission accomplished. Plus she stopped screaming. There, that wasn't so bad now, was it?

I joined Grandpa Dave and Bradley. He looked at me and asked, "What took you so long?" Pride was winning out over honesty. How could I tell him about the wrestling match in the ladies room? All women are supposed to have that motherly instinct, able to change a baby in no-time flat. I was not that woman. I was a granny school dropout. If I passed Diapers for Dummies 101, it was by a very slim margin.

Next question, "What's that smell." Fighting tears, I shared my nightmare: no changing table, no paper towels, no baby-wipes, the poop on my fingers, no soap. He started laughing. That didn't help. I burst into tears. Then Cassie started crying again. The more we cried, the more Dave laughed. Could this possibly be the same man I had fallen in love with? Where was his compassion?

Forget lunch. With every whiff of food, I fought off more waves of nausea. I ordered a cup of coffee and watched all of them eat. Cassie was finally happy and pleasant. Of course she was. Her little butt was clean. She was going to see Mickey Mouse with her

The Art of Grandparenting

brother, her granddad and this strange new friend of his. What could be better than that? She may have forgotten the whole mess, but my queasy tummy lingered on.

We did manage to go to the park. Since Dave's home was not too far away, we stopped by and I cleaned up a bit. The kids would have been so disappointed if we didn't go. The trip turned in to a magical day at Disney World after all.

But you, the person reading this chapter, the soon-to-be, or brand-new grandparent, let my words be fair warning. Memorize these valuable tips:

Beware of the 'other' grandma. She may deliver more than just the baby!

When dining out with baby, be positively certain that the restaurant has a changing table, preferably one with a seat belt! Check before you are seated. If they don't have one, go to another restaurant!

Check the diaper bag for baby-wipes, plenty of diapers and clean clothes.

Rubber gloves are recommended but optional.

Never, ever stick your fingers down the back of a baby's pants if there is a strong aroma of poop.

Dave and I enjoyed a two year courtship, before setting the date for our wedding. There were additional trips to Disney and other outings with the grandkids. My grand-parenting skills improved with practice.

About a week before our marriage, Dave's oldest daughter, Dana, asked permission for her two children to call me Grandma—no 'step-stuff'. Of course, there were Grandma responsibilities that I'd be expected to uphold too. I wept for joy and she cried right

THE ART OF GRANDPARENTING

along with me. In my previous marriage, I had not been blessed with children. This joyous request changed that fact forever—I finally have a family to call my own. Grandchildren! This was indeed a true Cinderella story, and I felt like the main character!

My grandchildren and I survived those early, inexperienced days, where I had no idea what I was doing. I have since learned that there actually is a "Grand Parenting for Dummies" book. I wondered if it might have helped with my first diaper changing melodrama. Hey, it was much more fun learning by fire! I'm a seasoned Grandma now.

I just want to close with a beautiful story my grandson, Bradley shared with me, when he was about five years old. We were in the car (it always seems like we're in the car with the kids!), and he shared that he had three grandmas. I said, "You do?" He proudly told me that Grandma Miller was Daddy's mother, and Grandma Helms was Mommy's mother, an angel in heaven. When God needed her up there, He gave them another grandma—"That's you, Grandma Gerri." And here I thought that God was answering my prayer. Maybe He was answering theirs too.

I don't get to spend as much time with my grandchildren as I'd like. They live about a thousand miles from me. They're older now too, on the cusp of their teens. At Easter, however, my grandson blessed me by asking if I'd stand up with him for his Confirmation at church. I was honored and proud to do it. As the priest prayed over the children, I stood behind this handsome, thirteen-year-old boy with my hands on his shoulders. He leaned his head back on me and I thought my heart would burst with joy. I look for the good in them, praise them for their successes and wins and try to overlook their few shortcomings. The joy they bring far outweighs the learning curve frustrations of when I first became their Instant Grandma.

the Art of Grandparenting

Tips & Tricks

Beware of the 'other' grandma. She may deliver more than just the baby!

When dining out with baby, be positively certain that the restaurant has a changing table, preferably one with a seat belt! Check before you are seated. If they don't have one, go to another restaurant!

Be sure any and every diaper bag has baby-wipes, plenty of diapers and clean clothes.

Rubber gloves are recommended but optional.

Never, ever stick your fingers down the back of a baby's pants if there is a strong aroma of poop.

Your grandchildren will survive your inexperienced days as a new grandparent.

Remember, your grandchildren are the answers to your prayers, and maybe, just maybe, you are the answer to theirs!

How to Become a Go-To Grandma

Donne Davis

I'VE HAD FOUR WONDERFUL GRANDMOTHER ROLE MODELS—my own two grandmas, who were a strong presence in my life from the day I was born until I was forty, and my mother and mother-in-law, the grandmothers of my two children. My paternal grandma came to the United States from Lithuania in 1936. After she learned English, she and my grandpa opened a retail store that was the family business for the next fifty years. She was a successful working woman, as well as the matriarch of our large family.

My maternal grandma, a native San Franciscan, was my best friend. I loved spending the night at her apartment and going on Saturday outings downtown or to the movies. She and my grandpa came to our house for dinner every Thursday. While my mom cooked dinner, my grandma and I would sit on the kitchen floor playing jacks together. When I graduated from high school, my grandma and I took a three-week train trip across the United States. Both of my grandmas were loving women and showered me with their love. They were gracious, devoted to their family, and had lots of friends. They both had spirit and spunk.

The Art of Grandparenting

Both of my grandmothers were "Go-To Grandmas."

What do I mean by a "Go-To Grandma?" And why should you want to become one? A GTG is the grandma your children can count on to be there when they call; the one they feel safe leaving in charge of their children; the one they turn to for help and support for the whole family; the one whose shoulder they can cry on when they can't take another minute of being a parent; the one who respects the parents' choices and validates all the hard work they're doing to raise your precious grandchildren.

You want to become a GTG so you can develop a bond with your children and your grandchildren that will last a lifetime. In my six years as a grandma I've learned a lot about how to balance my own needs and desires as a grandma with the needs of my daughter and son-in-law. The most important thing I've learned is that getting time with your grandchildren requires building trust and respect with their parents. Trust is the foundation for having access to your grandchildren. If there are any unresolved issues in your relationships with your children, they're going to come up as you develop a relationship with your grandchild. Here are some suggestions for ensuring your place as a GTG.

1. Commit to being there.

This first step is critical because it sets the tone, for hopefully, a long and loving relationship with your children and grandchildren. You want to get off to a good start, but it's going to take sensitivity and diplomacy. Listen carefully to what the new parents are saying before the birth and you'll pick up clues about what you can request.

Before you talk with your children, consider how much time you can devote to visits. You will need to juggle your responsibilities and it will alter your life, but the payoff is worth the effort.

Maybe you've given some thought to how often you'd like to see your new grandchild. Many factors determine the feasibility and frequency of your visits: the physical distance between you and your grandchild, your relationship with the parents of your new grandchild; your role as the maternal or paternal grandparent; everyone's work schedule.

Discuss with the new parents what they expect of you and what you expect of them, what help they would like and what help you can give. Be specific about this topic and use your negotiation skills. This is one of the most important conversations you will have. It will show your commitment to the new relationship with your grandchild.

Once you've decided what you're able to commit to, then begin a conversation with the new parents about everyone's wishes and expectations for the frequency and location of visits. This issue will also evolve as the baby gets older and the parents settle into a routine and schedule.

Not all new parents handle the early days following the birth the same. Some new parents prefer to bond with their newborn by themselves and don't want anyone else present. Be patient and understanding of their need to create and nurture their new family unit. This will be your first test of whether you can put aside your own needs and ego. You may have to accept what arises for you as a new grandma. Remember, that the more you push for what you want, the more the new parents will push you away.

Other new parents will welcome all the help they can get and will let you know their plans up front. If you can be there in those first few days after the birth, consider it an honor. You'll be the lucky grandparent who watches in awe as this tiny human being completely enchants and entertains you.

If you're fortunate enough to be invited to witness your child give birth, I encourage you to accept the invitation. It is truly a miraculous experience. My daughter invited me to be present at

The Art of Grandparenting

both of her deliveries and I felt truly blessed. Although I delivered both of my own children without anesthesia, I could not actually see them being born. Watching a baby emerge from the womb is both fascinating and awe inspiring. All the words that have been written about being a new grandma will now resonate with you. And you'll have a whole new set of your own feelings that cover the entire spectrum of emotions.

My daughter read a book called *HypnoBirthing* during her pregnancy and chose that method for its quiet, relaxed, natural birth. I learned to use a new set of vocabulary words, such as *surges* and *pressure*, to replace the familiar negative vocabulary of *labor* and *pain* associated with traditional childbirth. On the day my daughter gave birth to her first child, my husband and I arrived to find her draped over a giant exercise ball. Her head was resting on the arm of the living room sofa. She was having powerful *surges* and asked us to whisper while we were in the room. We all took turns massaging her lower back to try and bring her some comfort.

My daughter hired a *doula* to coach her throughout the pregnancy and help her prepare for birth. A doula is an assistant who provides various forms of non-medical support during prenatal care, childbirth and/or during the postpartum period. My daughter's doula almost missed the birth! My daughter wanted to stay at home for as long as possible and she did. We raced to the hospital and my daughter went straight into the delivery room where the doula met us.

I remember standing at the foot of my daughter's hospital bed, holding my breath as she gave one more push. Then this wet little head emerged. The midwife lifted it up and I saw that the baby's eyes were wide open! I looked into those eyes and she looked right back. It was the most miraculous moment of my life. In that moment I felt an incredible bond forming between my granddaughter and me. I remember leaping off the ground in total ecstasy. For the next few days it felt as if my feet would never touch the ground again.

The Art of Grandparenting

After my granddaughter's birth, my husband and I decided we wanted to visit her twice a month. We proposed it to them and they were thrilled. My daughter and son-in-law live about a two-hour drive away. We were committed to making the trip. Over the past six years we've been able to honor our commitment. I refer to our two-night visits as my "48-hour love fest."

2. Get on board with the parents' program.

Things have changed since we raised our children. New parents today have access to a vast amount of information. They have new ideas about childbirth, delivery, and parenting styles. While some expectant mothers want home births, many want to schedule an induced labor in the hospital so they can plan for the delivery.

I share my personal story because, if you want to have access to your new grandchild, you will need to be open and receptive to your children's parenting "program." There are new theories, equipment—car seats, strollers, co-sleepers—and styles of childrearing today.

Despite all this wealth of information, new parents still have lots of insecurities. However, they probably won't admit them to you. They want you to see them as competent. They need you to be supportive, observant and complimentary. But let's face it—you're all new at these roles. Sit down and discuss some of your questions in a non-judgmental way—it's a great place to begin your education. Express genuine interest in what they've been reading and learning.

Check out the Internet for a grandparenting class in your community. Many hospitals and medical centers around the country offer seminars to help new grandparents. They explain the latest obstetric and pediatric practices so grandparents can get up to speed and understand without having to ask or without having to challenge. Your children will be thrilled that you're taking your new role as a grandparent seriously.

The Art of Grandparenting

I had never heard of *attachment parenting* or *co-sleeping* before my granddaughter was born. Once I became familiar with the theories and witnessed the wonderful results, I was "on board" with their program. I've also become a believer in teaching sign language to babies, making your own baby food, and using new styles of discipline such as the popular "time-outs," also known as "thinking time."

3. Respect the parents' rules – don't be the disciplinarian.

One of the fascinating aspects of becoming a grandparent is the new relationship you'll have with your children. Your roles will now be reversed. Your children will be the ones making the rules and you'll be expected to follow them. Or at least try very hard to follow them, if you want time alone with your grandchild. I once let my three-year old granddaughter have a cookie and the first thing she did when we got home, was to run and tell her mommy! She was so excited she couldn't contain herself. My daughter forgave me but I didn't make that mistake again. It's going to get back to the parents and you're going to lose your credibility.

You will make mistakes as you adjust to the new parents' rules. Everyone is learning their new roles and nobody knows how they should behave. Our role, thankfully, is to **entertain, not enforce**. We did our stint as the disciplinarians when we raised our children, now we get to sit back and enjoy.

Warning: you may get complaints or feelings of envy from the parents when you're having so much fun that you're behaving like a child yourself. My daughter has told me on more than one occasion that she doesn't like being the Enforcer while I get to have all the fun. But that's another benefit of being a grandparent vs. a parent. We're not responsible for raising our grandchildren. Respecting your children's rules will guarantee you more face time with your grandchild and credibility as a GTG.

4. Don't give unsolicited advice.

Author Lois Wyse in her book, *Funny, You Don't Look Like a Grandmother*, has a short passage titled:

Grandmothers' Rights

Grandmotherhood does not give us

The right to speak

Without thinking,

But only the right

To think

Without speaking

Write this down and memorize it: *Think but don't speak.* If you don't follow any other steps but this one, you'll win the respect of your grandchild's parents. This is the simplest suggestion for becoming a GTG, yet the hardest to follow. One grandma I know says she's developed a blister on her tongue from biting it so often! That's a small price to pay for peace in the family.

Our children have a lot of new ideas about how to raise our grandchildren. If they're not causing them harm, you need to zip your lip and let them figure it out. That's what we did when we raised our children and they keep telling us "you did the best you could." If you absolutely can't stand it, find another grandma to commiserate with but make sure she's sworn to secrecy.

It takes time and patience to know when to come forward and offer help, and when to step back and say and do nothing. It's important to talk to your children about how they would like us to help them. Look for opportunities to verbally acknowledge the great parenting your children are doing, and be specific. For example, *I love the way you comfort the baby when she's crying.*

THE ART OF GRANDPARENTING

5. Get down on your grandchild's level – literally and figuratively.

Have you been telling yourself it's time to get in shape? Now you have the best motivation you could ask for. If you want face time on the floor with your grandchild, make a commitment to improve your strength and flexibility. It's not just for your own sake; now, it's for your grandchildren.

Walking and yoga are two of my favorite forms of exercise and they've enabled me to play on the floor, climb on the slide, and carry my granddaughters around when necessary. If you just can't get down on the floor, bend down to their level or sit in a chair to talk to them so they can see your face.

Read what's developmentally appropriate for your grandchild. Learn what to expect at each new stage, so when you're together, you'll know what kinds of play to engage in. There are literally, millions of websites with "normal stages of human development." Your children will be excited to know that you're following your grandchild's development.

Helpful hint: never compare your grandchild's developmental accomplishments with your friend's grandchild or with another of your grandchildren. Also avoid saying, for example, "you were walking and talking by the time you were one!"

Pay attention to the suggested age range when you're buying toys, too. It's helpful to ask for recommendations from the parents when you're buying gifts for your grandchild. I once bought a musical reading toy for my granddaughter. I'm glad I asked my daughter what she thought of it first. She asked me to return it because it looked too much like a computer and she didn't think it was appropriate for a two-year old. I respected her decision.

6. Create rituals for bonding with your grandchild.

Remember the bedtime rituals you had with your own children? Or the special ways you celebrated birthdays or holidays? Now you can create rituals with a new generation. Rituals are important for young children. They provide comfort and security for children. Rituals help children deal with change. They give them a sense of identity and an understanding of what is valued in their family. I grew up in a family that valued rituals and traditions. I passed them on to my children and now my daughter and son-in-law are creating new ones for their two daughters.

Rituals are different from routines. Routines create continuity. Rituals create connection. Rituals are the glue that bonds families together. When we do a ritual, we send a message saying: what we're doing matters and is meaningful to us. Repeating the ritual reinforces the bond that is created. Rituals don't have to be serious, solemn or centuries old to have an impact. They can be as simple as doing a group hug at the end of the day or a special way of saying goodbye to each other in the morning.

If you like to sing, choose one of your favorite children's songs to sing to your grandchild. Make it your signature song and sing it whenever you visit. Make up a special greeting or pet name for your new grandbaby and use it frequently with your own special hugs and kisses.

When my granddaughter was little, she always felt sad when I was ready to leave. On one occasion she came out to my car and looked in the glove compartment. She found a package of crackers and asked if she could have them. And thus our "goodbye ritual" was born. Now, whenever I leave, Juliet and her little sister Amelia, both run out to my car and search the glove compartment for their goodbye cracker treat.

Rituals are gifts of love you can give your grandchildren in the simplest of ways. All the special pet names you've given them add to their sense of identity. Every hug and greeting you shower them with contributes to their sense of security. Your very presence in their lives shows you value them. Pay attention to those simple rituals because they truly are the glue that bonds families.

7. Connect with other grandmas.

As a new grandmother, you will feel a flood of new emotions and wonder if you're normal for having them. Let me assure you that you are normal and you are not alone. Some grandma issues are universal—the good *and* the bad. You may feel envious of the other grandmother, fearful that you may drop your new grandchild, worried that your children have made some strange decisions, and a whole host of other feelings. Checking it out with other grandmas is comforting. I've swapped some adorable grandchildren stories with other grandmas on gift giving, toilet training, conversations with edgy, sleep-deprived parents and much, much more.

As a new grandma, I had so many questions I wanted to ask other grandmas, I decided to start an organization for enthusiastic grandmas like myself. I called it the GaGa Sisterhood®. I wanted to find out what other grandmas were experiencing and get some helpful advice from more seasoned grandmas.

Seven months after my granddaughter was born, I invited all the grandmas I knew to my house to begin a conversation about what it means to be a grandma today. We sat in a circle in my living room and told stories about what our grandchildren call us and how we got those names; the great lengths we go, to see them; all the roles we juggle to make time for them; and most importantly, how we get along with their parents. There was so much to share and not enough time to dive into all of it. We all agreed to continue the conversation and we've been going strong for six years.

Our Sisterhood has grown to a camaraderie of friends who can laugh about the joys and challenges of being a grandma. We meet every other month in members' homes throughout the San Francisco

THE ART OF GRANDPARENTING

Peninsula. We've covered a wide range of topics over the years. Ultimately, we strive to be more enlightened grandmas so that we can continue to grow and stay connected with our grandchildren and their parents. I've come to appreciate that grandmas are a fascinating, multi-dimensional group of women engaged in many different aspects of life. They're joyful about this stage of their lives and they're fun to be around.

Now you're on your way to becoming a GTG. This new stage of your life is the most exciting and satisfying role you may ever experience. Indulge yourself in the joy of being a grandma. Savor it, because the months and years will fly by faster than ever. Build your foundation early and you will be blessed with more love than you ever imagined.

the Art of Grandparenting

Tips & Tricks

Commit to being there.

Get on board with the parents' program.

Respect the parents' rules – remember, they are the disciplinarians, not you.

Wait for a request for advice or information instead of giving unsolicited advice.

Get down on your grandchild's level—literally and figuratively.

Create rituals for bonding with your grandchild.

Connect with other grandmas.

Indulge yourself in the joy of being a grandma.

Taking the DISTANCE out of Long-Distance Grandparenting

Arlene S. Uslander

WHEN I FOUND OUT that my two-year-old grandson, Eric, and his parents were going to move 8,000 miles away from me, all the way to Guam, my reaction most closely matched that of a friend who told me, "If my grandchild moved that far away, I would absolutely die!" And I thought I would, from a *broken heart*. Perhaps you have had a similar experience—maybe not as great a distance as the other side of the world (I hope not, for your sake, and the grandchildren's!), but far enough away to make you envious of your friends whose grandchildren live within driving, or even walking distance.

For months before Eric left, every time I was with him, all I could think about was that soon, I *wouldn't* be with him, and I found it difficult to sleep or eat or concentrate. Yet, when the time finally arrived and he left, I began to realize that there was nothing I could do to change the situation—that the only thing I could change was *my reaction* to the situation. So I stopped feeling sorry for myself, and started thinking more about my grandchild, and what I could do to make the transition as easy for him as possible.

The Art of Grandparenting

First of all, I did two things that a friend, who happens to be a family therapist, suggested, which you might want to try if your grandchild, or grandchildren move away:

1) Pack up a box of toys from your house that your grandchild especially liked, and send them to his or her new address, so the child will still feel a connection to *your house*.

2) Buy a small photo album (I bought one with Mickey Mouse on the cover) and take pictures of the family—including your pets, of course, if you have any—as well as of certain things in or around your house that your grandchild was fond of: a musical Teddy bear, a toy ice cream truck, books that you read to the child at bedtime, a game or two, etc., and write a caption under each picture. (Always the school teacher, I speculated that maybe those captions would help Eric learn to read?) According to my son, the toys and books from my house and the little photo album made a solid hit with Eric!

After Eric moved away, I found, both by comparing notes with other "long distance grandparents" and by trying my own ideas, that there are many things one can do to keep the relationship between you and your grandchildren alive and well. Here are some other ideas that worked well for me:

Audio cassettes

These can be used in many different ways, and your grandchildren can play them over and over again.

Shortly after Eric moved away, I sent him a cassette, which I called "Eric's Friends," on which I recorded the voices of people who were important to him at the time. Some of the people I recorded in person; others I taped over the phone, by purchasing an inexpensive phone-recording device. Each person said something different, to remind Eric of the special times they had shared together, and at the end of the message, he or she would ask, "Do you know who this is?" so it would be like a little game for him.

THE ART OF GRANDPARENTING

You can read story books on the cassette, and mail the book, along with the cassette, so your grandchildren can turn the pages and look at the pictures as they hear you read the story, or if they are old enough, to follow the words, themselves, as you read them aloud. Even though today, IPODS are the big deal, you can still buy cassette recorders/players. I know because I just bought one to record stories for my latest grandchild, who is two and a half years old. Obviously, you need to make sure that your grandchild (or grandchildren) also has a cassette player—or how else can he or she listen to your tapes? If the child doesn't have one—well, what are grandparents for?

Video tapes

Whoever invented the video camera (or the Webcam, as discussed later) must have been a "long distance grandparent." If you can't see your grandchildren in person, and they can't see you, the next best thing is seeing each other on video. If you don't own a video camera, try to borrow or rent one.

When Eric was little, video cameras used to be much larger and more cumbersome, and much more expensive than they are today. They now sell video cameras in stores that can fit in your purse or pocket.

Eric turned two a month after he moved away, and knowing that we couldn't be with him to celebrate his birthday, I gathered the whole family together to make a "Happy Birthday" video. We all wore birthday hats, including the two family dogs; we sang to him, and recited his favorite nursery rhymes and stories. Making the video gave us the feeling that we were part of Eric's birthday celebration even though we are 8,000 miles away. I continued to make video tapes of the family every time we got together for a holiday, and, of course, each of us always had a special message for Eric.

The Art of Grandparenting

Ask someone to video tape you reading story books aloud, and send the child the book along with the video tape—although today, you would be more likely to send DVD disks (digital video disks). Like audio cassettes, DVD disks can be played over and over again, as often as your grandchildren wish to see them. I have many video tapes of Eric, and of two of my other grandchildren Ryan and Carly when they were little, which I intend to have converted into DVD disks one of these days.

Webcams

What a wonder of technology these are! I only wish they had been on the market when all my grandchildren were little. In case you haven't heard of them, a Webcam, also called a homecam, is a video camera, usually attached directly to the computer, that sends images over the Internet. Ranging in price from as little as $39, to $100 or more, Webcams may or many not come with a microphone; so if you buy one, make sure it has one. Both you and your grandchild's parents need to have a computer and a Webcam in order to make this work.

When you both turn on your Webcams and follow the instructions that come with it, you will not only be able to see your grandchild moving around or just sitting in front of the computer, on your screen, but with the microphone attachment, you will be able to speak to, and hear each other talk. I believe that originally, the Webcam was invented to be used in business—visual and audio conference calls, for example. But, it did not take long before some ingenious person (most likely, a long-distance grandparent!) realized what a wonderful device the Webcam is for making it possible to see and talk to your grandchildren (and/or their parents), as though you were in a visual chat room—even if your grandchildren are thousands of miles away—and even if the sound on the other end is just babbling, which, of course, will be "music to your ears."

THE ART OF GRANDPARENTING

When Eric was a youngster, there was no such thing as a Web-cam, but today, using the Web-cam, a device you attach to your computer so that you can see and talk to your grandchildren on the computer screen, and vice versa, is an absolutely fantastic way to say in touch. Check out Webcams at your closest electronics store.

Photographs

Photographs, of course, are one of the best ways to take away some of the distance. I continued to send Eric photos of the people and things he most enjoyed back in Chicago, where we lived, and where he spent his first two years of life, as well as pictures that were taken of him and my husband and me together before he left. After he came to visit, which he did every summer, I sent him a small photo album filled with photos of things and places he saw in Chicago, and of the things we did together. I also sent him an 8-by-10-inch photo of my husband and me, which his parents hung in his bedroom. Not much chance of your grandchildren forgetting you if they see your face on the wall *every single day.*

Once digital cameras came out, my husband and son both bought one. Sending photos back and forth via the computer is also a wonderful way to stay in touch and to feel like you are part of your grandchild's special occasions and events, as you look at the photos right before your eyes on the computer screen.

Gifts

Gifts certainly will help keep you in your child's thoughts, and they don't have to be expensive. Even if you're not too handy with crafts (as I'm not), you can make simple things that appeal to children: sock puppets, yarn dolls, and little houses or farms from shoe boxes or other small boxes, for which you can purchase inexpensive animals, dolls, cars and trains at discount stores.

The Art of Grandparenting

Find out about little things your grandchildren want and send them in colorfully wrapped packages. Whenever you send your grandchildren a gift, ask their parents to show them your picture, so they know that the gift came from you.

Phone calls

Phone calls from you will be important, to you, as well as your grandchild. When you talk to your grandchild, mention the names of people and things with which he or she is familiar. Repeat the child's name and the name he or she calls you, several times during the conversation. Even if your grandchildren are too young to carry on a real conversation with you, they are *not* too young to listen.

Visits

Naturally, nothing can take the place of visits—you to your grandchildren, or your grandchildren to you. How often these visits take place will depend on individual circumstances—finances, work schedules, other family commitments, etc.

When you do visit your grandchildren, or they visit you, try to arrange special times to spend with them, *without their parents*. This will help you and your grandchildren become reacquainted, and will also give the parents some time to themselves—for which they will be very grateful. Take the children to places they especially enjoy, and to places they have never been. And, be sure to arrange for quiet time in the house to be alone with each child: to read stories, exchange confidences, and to give some extra hugs and kisses.

Emailing

As the children get older, and learn how to use a computer (and today, they are almost born knowing how to use a computer!), emailing is the best thing ever invented to connect grandparents and grandchildren who live apart. As Eric, and then his younger sister, Carly, got older, and I would get an email from them that said, "Dear Nagga (their special name for me) XOXOXOXO. Please write back," I was filled with joy! Also, don't forget the fax machine, if you have one. I will never forget the time I received a fax from Eric (dictated to, and written by one of his parents) that said, "I will sing one hundred songs for you." He was three years old then. I am still waiting!

Thank goodness, Eric and Carly no longer lives 8,000 miles away. But, there is still a geographic distance between us — *about half a block!* We all now live in Sonora, California. When my husband retired in September of 2008, we decided it was time to move here, since the grandchildren's parents were not about to leave this great community and move back to Chicago.

I won't pretend that I didn't wish Eric and Carly, and the "newcomer on the block," their little brother, Levi, lived closer to me; I missed them terribly. But soon after Eric moved away as a two-year-old, I realized that I had two choices: to feel sorry for myself (envying those friends whose grandchildren lived "down the street," or in the next suburb), or to put that negative emotional energy into the more positive, constructive attitude of viewing long-distance grandparenting as a creative challenge — a challenge to think of things to do for and with my grandchildren that would keep me in their thoughts, and prayers. I chose the latter, knowing that "out of sight, out of mind" is only true if you let it be.

I hope that if you are a long-distance grandparent, you, too, can learn to meet the challenge, and keep the connection between you and the children strong and deep.

the Art of Grandparenting

Tips & Tricks

Record and send audio cassettes or CDs.

Record and send video DVDs.

Get a Webcam and learn how to use it.

Take lots of pictures and send them via Internet.

Send inexpensive or homemade gifts.

Use frequent phone calls to hear each other's voices.

Visits are irreplaceable, if you can afford to travel to your grandchildren's new home.

Emailing is the fastest way to keep in touch.

Grandma's Kaleidoscope

Mary Pansini La Haye

"**I love you Grandma.**"

"And, honey, I love you."

Holding a baby as carefully as a piece of Waterford crystal, I look at my husband with his loving smile and his blue eyes, bluer than ever, gazing at the miracle of his granddaughter. This long-anticipated moment—with all the excitement of waiting—this moment in time is one to hold in the cradle of your heart.

I am a grandmother of six girls and three boys that range in age from four to thirty. They are all different. They go to high school, preschool, and college. They have careers and life partners. Through all of the growing and growing pains, I have laughed, cried and watched with worry and pride as each of them has navigated his or her way through life. With all my joys of being a grandmother, there is one that is missing—my husband did not live to see all nine of our grandchildren. He only met one. But I do have the memory of him holding our first granddaughter—the experience of her birth that we shared with so many relatives and friends.

The Art of Grandparenting

Waiting and waiting and finally the proud daddy came into the hall and announced, 'It's a girl."

The hallway was no longer a quiet zone. All of the births were exciting—and the image of seeing my own children as they gazed down at their newborns is something to treasure. The feeling of joy and pride I felt as my newborn granddaughter reached up to grab my son's finger and the look on his face is something I'll never forget.

As a child, I loved the mysterious whirling of a kaleidoscope. The patterns, shapes and colors come into focus and then change as quickly as they appear. Each spin brings a new pattern, a new image. Always changing. Always unpredictable and unexpected. Life is very much like a kaleidoscope. Bits and pieces of different shapes and colors don't look like much individually, but when put together they transform into a beautiful picture. Like a kaleidoscope, my memories have filled my mind with a mosaic of colorful life images. Let's give it a spin, and see what comes into focus.

First, every human needs a rocker, especially parents and grandparents. In the back and forth rhythm of the rocker two hearts beat as one. As they rock back and forth, the love of two people, years apart, are captured in moments of going off to dreamland. Sitting in a chair where drifting off seems natural. The seemingly endless moments of dreaming, singing and the fun of reading and enjoying the motion are all provided by one simple piece of furniture. But the day does come when the child is too big to jump into grandma's lap for a story, but then comes the happy day when the child is reading a story to you by looking at the colorful illustrations. They smile and laugh and give you a hug. When I was growing up, I remember the main picture on our living room wall—a reproduction of Renaissance

The Art of Grandparenting

artist, Rafael's "Madonna of the Chair." The Madonna, sitting in the chair has a child on her lap and another standing at her shoulder. The look on her face is one of happiness and peaceful contentment. Appreciate the chair.

Spin the kaleidoscope. Parties, parties, parties! I have attended birthdays, graduations, and pool parties, beach parties all with children, teenagers, music, noise, sugar, tears, laughter and friendships. Here is what I've learned. I don't like sushi but I ate it on the occasion of a graduation. I do like old-fashioned, grilled hamburgers on the Fourth of July. Two-year-olds are scared of the Cookie Monster and a child's first haircut does qualify for a big celebration. Each party marks important life cycle events—each and every one is as important as the next. Birthdays, especially the first birthday, seem to be important in our family. The child won't remember but the adults, who have the best time, certainly will. On first birthdays, I had a habit of making a special little one-layer cake with icing that soon spread all over the face and hands of the child of honor. They can eat it, spread it or push it all over their face—just as messy as they want. It's all theirs, to do what they want. The messier the merrier! (And the adults always have the cameras rolling!!) If you are a new grandparent, without a camera, stop reading this, and go out and get one right now!! And don't forget the rocker.

As grandparents, we have the privilege of experiencing all the "firsts" in a child's life just as we had with our children, but with a new and fresh perspective: The first smile and giggle, the first reaching out with their little arms, the first step as they walk to you, the first time they join a team, ride a bike or drive a car. Their first dates, their first days of high school, their first days on a new job. The freshness

The Art of Grandparenting

and excitement of all of life's firsts never gets old. How happy you will be in the celebration of all of the little and big accomplishments and the fun of hearing a grandchild try to form first words. It always seems to be a race between mama, dada, dog and banana. It may be awhile before they say grandma or nanny but it's worth the wait.

And then there is another wait before you hear, "I love you grandma!"

With that remark comes a grandparent's hugs and kisses and, "Oh honey, I love you too." How happy I am when I hear a grandchild's voice, no matter the age, on the phone. Thank you, Mr. Bell.

Oh, the holidays and holydays with all the food, packages and fun! The wonder of Christmas and Hanukkah, and special days of everyone's religious persuasion. The *ohs* and *ahs* of the Fourth of July, Halloween. All the birthdays, trips to the beach, running along the shore and smiling as the waves hit their little feet. A trip to the mountains where the sights and feel and sounds of tall pine trees reaching for the sky inspire awe. The making of their first snowball. As I sit and reminisce, so many of the details, the little things that never seemed memorable or important at the time, are the things that are now most focused, the things I remember the most. The pieces of the kaleidoscope are unraveling.

Spin the kaleidoscope. One summer day while sitting on my front porch, my ten-year-old granddaughter attempted to teach me a new card game. I patiently learned the rules, and then I was unkind enough to win.

She gathered up the deck and said, "I can't believe I let an old lady beat me!"

The Art of Grandparenting

I squealed with laughter! It was a good time to have a little discussion about the choice of words and what would be polite. And that was another different kind of moment to remember, a moment that defines the versatility of grandparenting. Last week that same grandchild, now a young lady in college, came by with a milkshake. We sat on the same front porch and talked about our lives while sipping the cold drinks. Appreciate milkshakes.

Recently I attended the wedding of my granddaughter. Travel was difficult and arrangements were overwhelming. But the moment I saw the bride walking down the hall, I was overcome with emotion. All these years, all the memories, all the images of the kaleidoscope came together at that very moment. There was my granddaughter, standing before me taking that next step, making a life of her own.

These children—my grandchildren—have grown to adulthood and are now in this world to shape their own lives, to make a difference and to rock their own babies and someday their own grandbabies. They are now confident in their own identities, the images of their kaleidoscopes are taking shape and will become their own. As we have lived this life with all of the joys and struggles, one of the greatest joys of being a grandmother is seeing adult grandchildren mature and transform from little dependent children into wonderful human beings. We've come a long way since that first lullaby in the rocking chair. Knowing that I had a hand in their lives and knowing that they will always be okay makes me feel whole and happy.

Thank you, God, for my children and grandchildren and may they always be in your shadow.

the Art of Grandparenting

Tips & Tricks

Get a rocking chair and appreciate the lasting memories the chair creates.

Make sure you have a camera to capture all the "firsts" and celebrations in your grandchildren's lives.

Use the phone and thank Mr. Bell for the invention that brings you closer to your grandchildren, no matter what the distances.

Play games with your grandchildren and sometimes let them win.

Do have discussions on being polite when a circumstance brings you the opportunity.

Appreciate the *milkshakes* your grandchildren bring to your life.

Remember, because you will have a hand in the lives of your grandchildren, you will know they will be okay.

Not What I Expected
Lessons of a New Grandmother

Sharon Bray

I BECAME A GRANDMOTHER FOR THE FIRST TIME when my grandson, Nathan, was born on February 6, 2009 in Pensacola, Florida. I'd looked forward to grandparenting long before his arrival, stopping to coo at other people's babies in supermarket aisles or wistfully lingering in infant wear departments. When my youngest daughter became pregnant, I eagerly volunteered my help as she took her first steps toward motherhood, just as I had in her first uncertain steps as a toddler. I embraced the impending title with all the enthusiasm I could muster. I never expected I would be caught off guard by the demands of my new role or that I would thrust into new learning as much, perhaps, my daughter was as a new mother.

In the first two weeks after Nathan's birth, I ran headlong into an emotional minefield. I returned home to San Diego with my pride noticeably wounded. It wasn't until I dared to mention my confusing experiences to a few friends that I discovered they were shared by others who had also become grandmothers. We'd been led to think that becoming a grandmother was natural, something we knew how to do by default. After all, we reared the sons and daughters

THE ART OF GRANDPARENTING

of our grandchildren, didn't we? Anything that had challenged our assumptions made us feel as if we'd missed something important in the grandmother how-to manual.

I write this essay for the expectant grandmother, the first-timer, the mother whose daughters will shortly give birth. I write because I wish I'd had a book like this one that would have offered me tips for navigating the terrain of my new role. Perhaps you'll encounter different hurdles than I did, but for those of you who have been mothers to daughters and are now soon going to be grandmothers to their children, I write to you.

I'm the mother of two daughters. I've enjoyed a close and affectionate relationship with each of them. As Claire became a mother, I eagerly embraced the role of grandmother. But I was caught completely off guard by the need to reconfigure the mother in myself. I didn't expect to have to swallow the bitter pill that my sage advice might be cast aside for the rockier terrain of trial and error. I didn't expect that I would feel the same contradictions and awkwardness as the mother of a new mother as I had during her adolescent years: "Hold me tight. Let me go. Please help. You're in the way." I hadn't expected any of it. Who would?

I believed, like many mothers, that I would one day be a grandmother. I imagined photographs of my many grandchildren tucked into my wallet. I'd receive dozens of greeting cards emblazoned with "world's best grandmother" on the front. My refrigerator would be adorned with my grandchildren's artwork. What's more, I wasn't about to be some doddering old grandparent; I planned to be youthful in appearance, energetic and fun. "Hey," I imagined the teenaged friends of my grandchildren saying, "Your grandma's way cool."

THE ART OF GRANDPARENTING

It wasn't until I turned sixty that I was forced, by the reality of advancing age, to re-evaluate my expectations. My daughters' most fertile years were quickly diminishing, as was the population of marriageable young men. I reluctantly considered the possibility I might not have any grandchildren at all if they didn't find true love soon. "Relax," my husband said, "It will happen."

For the next two or three years, both girls continued to bring boyfriends home to us, but if I dared ask, "So, any plans for...?" I was greeted with rolling eyes and an exasperated, "Oh Mom..." When Claire suddenly made the decision to uproot herself and move to Florida at age 36 to continue an online romance, I was flabbergasted.

"You met him online?" I gasped, imagining some sexual pervert at the other end of her computer.

"Oh Mom," she sighed, "You've been watching too many *Law and Order* re-runs."

My more sophisticated high-tech friends concurred. Online romances were common among younger adults. I held my breath and helped her pack up her belongings. When she experienced a mild panic attack the night before her move, I held her in my arms and said, "You have to follow your heart," hoping the anxiety I was feeling for her did not show. I lacked the power to save my daughters from the mistakes I'd made when it came to men. I crossed my fingers, kissed her good-bye as she left for the airport and burst into tears as the car disappeared around the corner.

A few months later, Claire flew home to California with Mark, the man who won her heart. He was a sharp contrast to all her old boyfriends and another assault on my expectations. He was forty, previously married and the father of three children under the age of ten, but I liked him immediately. A year later, Mark called me from Florida.

The Art of Grandparenting

"Sharon," he cleared his throat. "I've called to ask for your blessing," he stammered. "I'm going to ask Claire to marry me."

I squealed with excitement. "Of course," I managed to say.

Just a year later, Claire called with the news. "We're having a baby," she announced. I nearly dropped the telephone. "Mom? Did you hear what I said?" I'd heard it all right. Tears were streaming down my face.

"Oh honey," I began. "I'm…" and unable to say much more for the lump clogging my throat, I squeaked, "so happy. Thank you."

When you hear your daughter say the words, "we're having a baby," for the very first time, there is an overwhelming rush of emotion unlike any experienced before. Perhaps it's something about continuity, but you fall in love with that nascent life the minute you hear it exists. Watching a daughter prepare for motherhood has a special magic, but it is also accompanied by the resurgence of your own motherly instincts: pride, protectiveness, and worry.

Claire was well past the optimal age for conception. Worry hovered in the background at every stage of her pregnancy. I anxiously awaited each test result. I tried not to show concern as her medical record bore ominous labels like "elderly gravitas" and "advanced maternal age." I prepared myself for the possibility that this new life might not live to full term, be normal or healthy. I vowed to love this new little being no matter what. It was impossible to do otherwise.

Claire shared her progress with me in weekly telephone or video-conference calls. I received copies of every sonogram documenting fetal development. I breathed more easily as her pregnancy passed the first three months, when the majority of miscarriages occur. I listened attentively as she temporarily obsessed over research on autism, Down's Syndrome, and a host of other potential risks that are known to increase with maternal age.

"You're doing great," I'd say cheerily. "It's going to be just fine."

THE ART OF GRANDPARENTING

Yet after each call, I sent dozens of silent prayers heavenward. "Please, please let the baby be healthy."

I never confessed any of my own worries. I couldn't. *I* was Claire's cheerleader, her mother, the one who soothed her childhood fears. I embraced this new stage of our mother-daughter relationship with the zealousness of a football coach whose team is tied in the final quarter. I vowed to be by her side at every step of her nascent motherhood. After all, I was the voice of experience.

Medically, Claire was in good hands. Because of her age and other risk factors, she was given extra attention and referred to a high risk pregnancy specialist who won her trust. As the birth grew near and the baby's size increased to over nine pounds, an induced delivery was necessary. ("I don't know what you're feeding that baby," her doctor said, "but he's got to get out.") I began making travel plans.

"How long can you stay?" My daughter asked, her voice sounding eerily like the eight-year-old daughter whose knees I lovingly bandaged. My heart banged against my chest.

"As long as you need me," I replied in as reassuring a voice as I could muster. "Mother to the rescue," I murmured. An image of Wonder Woman flitted across my mind. I booked a round trip ticket to Florida for a two week stay and cleared my calendar for the entire month of February, just in case.

On February 6, 2009, I boarded the flight that took me from San Diego to Pensacola. I was in a state of nervous excitement. Claire's obstetrician had moved the induction procedure ahead earlier than originally planned, and it appeared that my arrival would coincide with my grandchild's.

During my layover in Dallas, I paced the terminal in a state of agitated frustration. I called my son-in-law. "How is she?"

"She's doing great," he replied. "She's walking around." I made the second call as I was boarding my flight to Pensacola. "Eight centimeters dilated."

I practically danced onto the airplane. The flight was just an hour and a half in duration, but I felt like storming the cockpit and shouting at the pilots, "Can't you move this thing any faster? I'm about to be a grandmother."

The moment we landed, I punched in the number for Mark's cell phone. Voicemail. "You've reached," the recording began. It meant only one thing: the baby was on his way.

"Let's go," I motioned to my sister-in-law, who'd met me at the gate. We sprinted to the parking lot. As I climbed into the passenger's seat of her SUV, I remembered my suitcase, left to rotate indefinitely on the conveyor belt. I jumped out of the car and raced back to claim it. I ran back to the car with my bag swaying precariously behind me. As we exited the airport and turned toward town, my cell phone rang.

"Hello?" My heart was pounding.

"We have a beautiful, healthy boy," Mark said, his voice full of emotion.

I shrieked, startling my sister-in-law, who braked the car sharply, sending her gift for the new parents, a decorative fruit basket, skidding across the backseat. Half of the melon flowers disintegrated on impact. "Sorry," I gushed. "He's here." I wiped the tears from my eyes. "How fast can you get to the hospital?"

Be ready to fall apart when your grandchild is born. It's a double whammy to your heart. There is the fact of the baby, your grandchild, and the sheer miracle of life, but there is something else, something I didn't anticipate. Nothing—and I mean nothing—prepares a mother for the sight of her daughter suddenly transformed into a mother.

As I tiptoed into the delivery room, all I saw was Claire, her eyes rimmed red with exhaustion and emotion. She was more beautiful in that moment than she ever had been. In her arms lay a perfect little boy, his tiny mouth firmly latched onto her breast. She looked up at me and smiled. "Look what we made, Mama."

I gazed at her through a mist of tears and bent to kiss her cheek. Wasn't it just yesterday that I cradled her in my arms?

"Do you want to hold him?" Of course I wanted to hold him, but for a moment I wanted only to take it all in, to look at her, a mother, with her son.

"He's beautiful," I murmured. "And you're beautiful," I added. She tenderly detached the baby from her breast and held him out to me. I had once been experienced at holding infants, but suddenly, it felt as if I'd forgotten everything I once knew. I felt clumsy and self-conscious as I took Nathan in my arms.

"Relax, Mama," Claire said softly. "You won't hurt him. He's your grandson." Our roles had reversed themselves. *She* was reassuring me.

In the weeks before Nathan's birth, I had sagely advised my daughter to be prepared for the roller coaster ride of emotions during her first days as a new mother. Here was the first surprise: as a new grandmother, I was just as vulnerable to emotional upheaval. Time and again in the days that followed, a torrent of motherly emotions rose up and throttled me. My unruly feelings were as unpredictable as a wayward elevator.

Mark and Claire brought Nathan home two days later. Our plan was straightforward: on Monday, Mark would return to work, and I would be on hand to assist Claire as she adjusted to motherhood.

You know what they say about the best laid plans. "I think I'll ask for one more day off," Mark announced as I busied myself with

THE ART OF GRANDPARENTING

dinner preparations. I felt an immediate surge of tension, and silently chided myself for the primal tigress that had suddenly surfaced.

Claire looked up from nursing the baby, her face aglow. "Oh could you? That would be so great."

I felt myself receding into the background. Stay loose, I thought, trying to rise above my slightly wounded pride. It would only be one more day. I flashed my most beatific smile at my son-in-law. "What a fine idea," I said as enthusiastically as I could.

It was all the encouragement Mark needed. He picked up the telephone and punched in the number of his supervisor. I crossed my fingers behind my back. Surely he was desperately needed at the office.

"Gosh, are you sure? Thank you so much," he said. Uh oh, I didn't like the sound of what I was hearing.

"Hey, I got the entire week off," he grinned and kissed my daughter's cheek. I quickly did the calculations. Including the weekend, father, mother, son *and* grandmother would be together for all but two days of my stay. My stomach churned into a hard knot of resentment. I had flown all this way to help. Yet Mark *was* the father, I reminded myself. He *was* entitled.

I quietly set the table for dinner. A sliver of self-pity lingered. I had an elaborate mental image of days filled with tender moments for three: my daughter, grandson and me. I had inadvertently excluded my son-in-law from the picture. Now that Mark would be on hand 24/7, I was being forced into the wings. Suddenly, my role was reduced to a bit part.

Mark wasn't uninformed on the subject of mothers and newborns. He had already fathered three delightful children, a fact I'd conveniently overlooked. I've often joked that I was born on the cusp of June Cleaver and Gloria Steinem, but my assumptions made me look like a throwback to the era where men did not take as active a role in day-to-day parenting. I had neglected to remember just how engaged a father Mark is with his children.

This was, perhaps, the more obvious lesson of becoming a grandparent. I was not the parent, and I had one foot outside the primary family unit. I had veered into feeling as if I was in competition with my son-in-law for the lead role in a modern day version of which parent knows best. This was no contest: Mark was Claire's husband and Nathan's father. *I* was the extra on the set.

The days that followed were nothing like the tender scenes between mother, daughter and grandson I had envisioned. As Claire suffered sleep deprivation and unexpected difficulties with nursing, it wasn't me she turned to, but her calm and protective husband.

They made urgent trips to the pediatrician and the lactation specialists. "The what?" I asked, incredulous that breastfeeding had become a field of specialization. When supplemental formula was suggested as a stop-gap measure until Claire's milk supply increased, I watched aghast as my son-in-law mixed powdered formula with water from the refrigerator's filtered supply. "Shouldn't you boil that first?" I asked, fearing for my grandson's tender digestive tract. Neither Mark nor Claire appeared to hear my question.

"Shouldn't you put him in the bassinet to sleep for awhile?" My husband and I had given them a lovely, portable bassinet just for that purpose. "It will help establish a routine," I advised. The bassinet stood empty by their bedside. "Do you always nurse him whenever he wants?" My suggestions hung in the air, unheeded by either parent, and my advice was, politely, but firmly, ignored. I felt like I'd been born in the ice age. It seemed I knew precious little about modern-day infant care.

I was the loose edge of a well worn carpet that everyone stumbles over. Was I was providing any assistance beyond an elevated maidservant? Don't get me wrong, I *was* helping, but I not in the

The Art of Grandparenting

way I'd so meticulously envisioned. If I'd imagined I'd provide the training wheels, it appeared that these riders really didn't want them.

I began to manufacture excuses to run errands, anything to get me out of the house and away from the awkwardness I was experiencing. I became a regular at the local Wal-Mart, the major store in strip-mall-laden Navarre. (Ask me anything about that store, and I can now direct you to the appropriate aisle.) I was a woman without a mission. A player without a part.

Let's face it. I had my roles all mixed up. I may have become a grandmother, but I was struggling with being a mother to an adult daughter who had become a mother herself. In my mind, she was still my sweet baby girl, not the capable woman she had become. I was also new at another role: mother-in-law. I was the one who needed training wheels. I was back to trial and error learning all over again, and I was getting my knees scraped routinely.

Despite the bumpiness of this new territory, sooner or later, it was my turn to hold Nathan. My turn to rock him to sleep. My turn to examine his tiny fingers and toes, stroke his face, and feel the warmth of his body against my chest. In those moments, everything else melted away. Nothing existed but my grandson and me. It was Nathan who was teaching me how to become a grandmother.

For the last two days of my stay, I did have my daughter and grandson to myself, but I was hardly the able grandmother. I felt weepy and confused. "Gosh Mom," my daughter said as she embraced me at the airport. "I had no idea it would be so hard on you." Neither did I. All I wanted at that moment was to get on the airplane and get back to my world, where I knew my part and my lines were memorized. Yet as I handed over my sleeping grandson to his mother and walked toward the gate to board my flight back to San Diego, I felt as if my heart was being ripped out of my chest.

THE ART OF GRANDPARENTING

In the months since Nathan's birth, I have learned that being a grandmother means, among other things, playing whatever part is needed. I've learned how to take direction, not give it, to bite my tongue, to run with any new script thrust at me at the last minute or simply, to improvise. I'm learning that it's enough just to be on hand. It's enough to simply show up and be supportive as my daughter navigates her new role as mother to Nathan. I'm getting better at letting Claire and Mark be the parents they want to be, learning, as I did, by trial and error, but taking on the task with complete dedication and love. It doesn't get better than that.

I've also learned that I can be the grandmother I want to be in those cherished moments I have alone with Nathan. I cuddle and rock him to my heart's content. I play, make funny faces, talk baby talk, or sing silly songs that make him squeal with laughter. On my most recent visit to Florida, my daughter smiled as I danced with my grandson around the living room to Jimmy Durante's "Make Someone Happy."

"I think you're going to be his <u>fun</u> grandmother," she said.

I grinned from ear to ear. "Just call me Gram-a-rama," I said, thrilled at the designation.

I imagined Nathan agreeing. "Yeah," he'd nod his head, "my grandma is 'way cool."

the Art of Grandparenting

Tips & Tricks

Remember you are there to help make the transition into parenthood easier.

Include your son-in-law in the picture. He's going to be there, so remember you are the extra wheel on the cart.

Leave your hard-earned experience aside, and let your children learn the old-fashioned way: by trial and error. They may eventually ask your opinion.

You can be the grandparent you want to be when you are alone with the grandchildren.

If being *way cool* is your goal, then start at the beginning. Even if you have physical limitations, *way cool* has no boundaries.

Grandchildren: Your Reward for Raising Your Own

Tim Stewart

YOU SEE AN ADVERTISEMENT FOR SOMETHING, say, a new flavor of ice cream. The picture makes it look inviting. The words make it sound delicious. The whole presentation draws you in. You decide to try it. When you actually do, you find out that it is more wonderful than pictures or words could portray. The first bite brings sensations that you have never experienced before. The next bite is even better. Your mouth is watering at the mere thought of the next one. That is grandparenting.

You have seen your friends do it, and it looks good. You have heard people talk about it, and it sounds good. But, until you experience it yourself, you cannot understand how truly amazing it really is.

I would like to go back to that first moment I found out I was going to be a papa. I remember my first thought: *This is it. It is over. My life has reached the end and I didn't even see it coming.* My first vision was of my granddad. He was old. Old from the day I met him. I didn't want to be old. I had too many things left to accomplish in life. *Say it isn't so.*

Then, we got the call. She is in labor. We dropped everything and zoomed to the hospital. The memory of that day rushes back. With the exception of the births of my own children, this would become the greatest day of my life. When I got to hold Miss Kailyn Michelle Kiraly for the first time, I knew I could never give her up again. It was like waking up on Christmas morning to find everything you have ever wanted sitting under the tree. Your grandchildren are definitely your reward for putting up with your own.

As I held Kailyn that first day, my mind flashed back to raising my own children:

The bumps, the bruises, the regurgitated peas.
The warm summer evenings and the stormy seas.
The calm nights, sleepless nights, the nights without an end.
Like the story of the willow, thank God we learned to bend.
Santa and the Easter Bunny, the tooth fairy and a special elf.
Our life was lived for them with little thought of self.
Great memories. Sad memories. Memories I thought long gone.
They all came flashing back. And, I cherish them, every one.

I began to wonder how my little girl was going to be as a mommy. How could I teach her the lessons I had learned without being the over-bearing parent. Someone tried to take Miss Kailyn from my arms. I felt like a little boy again and someone was taking my favorite toy. I wasn't ready to give her up yet. Yet, I knew that if I let her go, she would come back to me. I quickly figured out the etiquette of babies. The last one to hold them got to hold them the longest. So, I would sit patiently while everyone else took their turn with my new little girl. Then, while they were making small talk, I

The Art of Grandparenting

would swoop in, scoop her up and move out of eyesight of the others. Out of sight, out of mind. I would look into her eyes, she into mine. I would sing softly to her. She would coo her approval. This was more than a reward; it was a gift straight from the heavens. This was that amazing taste that no words or pictures could put into perspective.

I have the good fortune to have repeated this scene four more times. Miss Taylor-Anne, Mr. James, Mr. Jesse and Mr. Ethan have joined Miss Kailyn as my brood. Each one of them special and unique in their own way. Each one a new flavor, different than the others, but equally amazing. Each one has carved out their own little section of Papa's heart. Each one has fallen asleep in Papa's arms. Each one has given the unconditional love that only babies and puppies can give. Each one has made me understand the true meaning in life. Family is first over everything else. We miss that message when we are young. We still want to do our own thing at times. We want to play basketball when they want a diaper changed. We want to go to a baseball game when they want to play Candy Land. We want to enjoy our vacation when they choose to express their own feelings of discomfort of being away from their safety net. Then, somewhere along the line, a change happens. It happens quicker for moms than dads. For moms, it is almost an immediate change. They get it with the first sound of the baby at the moment of birth. We dads can be a little slow on the uptake. But, eventually, we get it. It is the little things that mean the most. We shop for hours to find the right present for Christmas and they have more fun with the box than the gift. We plan for weeks for the perfect vacation, but they are happiest with that Saturday morning snuggle. There is no such learning curve for grandparents. It is immediate for both Nana and Papa. Family before all else.

There were times in my own children's lives that I wasn't able to be there. Maybe it was first grade concert or a county track meet, or

The Art of Grandparenting

some other event that conflicted with my schedule. There are no such conflicts with my grandchildren. I know my purpose. I now know why my grandparents were there when my dad was working. I know why my wife's parents were there when I was gone and I know that I will be available when my children have their own commitments to meet. It is the circle of life.

Quite often I tickle, tease, or do something silly with my grandchildren. When they ask me how I learned to that, the answer is always the same. I learned it in the Papa Manual. As they have gotten a bit older, especially Miss Kailyn, the say that there is no such thing. Well, now there is. Here are some excerpts from the First Edition of the Papa Manual written by, well you guessed it, Papa.

From the chapter titled, How, When and Where to Tickle Your Grandchildren.

Grandchild tickling is an art that has been passed on from Papa to Papa for many generations. Papas are required to tickle their grandchildren in many situations. For example, it is mandatory for a Papa to tickle a belly button any time it can be seen. This includes, but is not limited to: when they are not wearing a shirt, when their shirt lifts above the belly button when they raise their arms, when you lift their shirt to expose said belly button, and any other time the belly button is seen in public.

Papa tickling is always appropriate, regardless of what daughters, sons or grandchildren may say. Papas know when their baby needs a smile. It might be at the theater during a boring movie. It might be at a family reunion when all the big kids are playing their own game. It might be a wedding, a funeral, a family gathering or just a quiet night in the back yard. A papa knows it is time to tickle when his Papa Tickle Sense begins to tingle.

The Art of Grandparenting

From the Chapter Titled, Papa Storytelling.

Papa's stories are always the best and do not need to have some special moral or point that needs to be made. They can be as silly as a stork flying an airplane or a frog wearing flippers. They can be as fictional as fairy tale or as true as a documentary. The content or context of the story is no where near as important as the sound of Papa's voice in his baby's ears. Papa's stories are always appropriate, regardless of what daughters, sons or grandchildren may say.

From the Chapter Titled, Papa Singing.

The common theme from the first two chapters is that Papa singing is always appropriate, regardless of what daughters, sons or grandchildren may say. It does not matter if you are a trained tenor or a tone deaf dwarf; the sound of a Papa's voice in grandchildren's ear is like an angel in a meadow with a gently running brook near by.

There are far too many chapters of the Papa's Manual to reference in this letter, but understand, the Papa manual does exist. It may not be on a book shelf bound in red leather, but it is every bit as real. With every beat of a Papa's heart, a new word, phrase or chapter is being made. Every time you lock eyes with your grandbaby, or they reach their tiny arms up to you, another page is being made.

The Papa Manual is not something you read, it is something you live. As a papa, you have been a dad and a kid. You remember the things your papa did and how they drove your dad nuts. You remember the things your dad did, and even though it drove you nuts, it made your babies smile. Now, it is your turn. Put on your suspenders, hitch up your pants, grab your glasses, put in your false teeth and go out and spoil those new grandbabies. It is not just a

the Art of Grandparenting

good time, it is your Papa Duty. Your grandchildren are definitely your reward for putting up with your own.

I wish you only the very best in your experiences with the new additions to your family.

Tips & Tricks

It is normal to recall your parenting moments as you learn to grandparent your grandchildren.

You are writing every page in your very own, one-of-a-kind Papa Manual as you spend time with your grandkids. Use every page.

Tickling is great fun, especially belly buttons.

Singing is essential, no matter your abilities.

Storytelling is the realm for all grandpaarents, and especially Papas. Make up silly stories with or without messages in the tales.

Life Lessons

Chuck McCann

Honey, guess what? "Neither the excitement in her voice nor the glow on her face could hide her good news. "We're going to be grandparents." That little bombshell dropped into our lives within weeks of the wedding. We hadn't yet even finished the bottle of wine brought home from the wedding. "Isn't that wonderful?"

I agreed and continued hosing off the lawnmower. She went next door to tell the neighbors.

My daughter a parent. Oh boy.

Friends joked about incidents of grandparenting and the joys the little one brings into your life. Of course, they also made a very special comment, "You can always send them home." What did that mean? You don't want to know. Believe me you don't want to know. After a couple of hours with the grandchildren and they go home, you're exhausted. But you love them, and in some way try to enrich and teach them the lessons of life.

Perhaps there will come a day when children and grandchildren may wonder why parents or grandparents said or did something very

The Art of Grandparenting

differently from customary grandparent behavior. Perhaps something occurred when grandparents behaved in a manner unacceptable to the standard grandchildren expect. Knowing the story behind some of the things we did while our grandchildren were growing up might surprise you or might tickly your fancy, or leave you wondering if we were crazy to behave as we did.

Before I start the stories, you should know that I was married to a woman named Jean before I married Rita. The children from that first marriage are known to Rita's and my children as aunts and uncles. But, Jean's and my first child, Sandy, was born hydrocephalic. The day she died her head would not fit into a bushel basket. She lived exactly eighteen months, never walking a step in her life.

Sandy had the laugh of an angel. I came home from teaching school one day to hear her laughing, squealing with delight. Peeking into her room, Jean's dad, Jim, was picking up a squeak toy from the floor and dropping it on Sandy's belly as she lay in her buggy. Picking it up and dropping it over the edge of the buggy, she listened to the squeaking sound it made. She laughed and squealed each time she heard it. I have no idea how long Jim played this little game with Sandy, I only know that he didn't allow the tears cascading down his cheeks to interrupt Sandy's enjoyment.

My daughter Lyda, also from a previous marriage, had difficulty with school subjects and is the only kid I know who failed Driver's Education. She still cannot drive a car. Shortly after her mother died, she married a young man with a few problems, including drugs. We couldn't talk her out of the idea of marrying this fellow. Neither

THE ART OF GRANDPARENTING

could her stepfather. During the first few years, scattered between the many fights and separations, three children were born to Lyda and her husband. There were times when she asked us for money, which we refused to give her. But we would meet her to pay for medication and to see one or two of the grandchildren.

After one ugly fight, Lyda deliberately took an overdose of something. When questioned by the police at the hospital, she said there was no one to care for the kids. All three were placed into the DCFS program in Indiana. One time, when she went to court, we accompanied her, but we were never asked to enter the courtroom. The children remained in the care of DCFS. Unbeknownst to us, Lyda signed her eldest child and only son into institutional care. She gave up her two girls for adoption. As grandparents, our contact with them is gone. It is probably for the best.

Sitting in the kitchen, elbows on the table, sipping a cup of coffee, I found Rita's threatening fist shaking in front of my face. "I'm going to kill you," each word quietly bitten off as she said them.

Bewildered, for as far as I knew, I had done nothing to solicit this threat, I asked, "Why?"

"Listen."

Our granddaughter, Laura, was in the other room riding her hobbyhorse, singing some childish mish-mosh of some sort. Grandma Rita wanted me to listen to her sing—but why kill me for her singing? "What am I listening for?"

"Listen," she hissed.

The Art of Grandparenting

My hearing is not what it should be, so I strained to hear the words of the song. The melody was very sing-songy. In cadence with the rocking of the hobbyhorse she sang, "Somma dah beech," or some syllabic combination that sounded like that.

I repeated, "Why kill me?"

"She's singing *son of a bitch*. Singing it! You are the person who uses that expression often. Can you guess where she learned it?"

Laura wasn't punished for using the phrase, only asked not to sing it any more. As for me, I had to learn to use language unbecoming a gentleman with caution, or better yet, to change it. Changing didn't come easy.

I'll bet you can guess where I'm going with this, and you are right. At lunch, while spending the day with Rita and me, Laura dropped her spoon onto the floor. Attempting to reach for it without getting up, her arm brushed against her glass of milk. Milk splashed across the table and dripped onto her face, while she vocalized a clear and hearty "Oh shit." I guess I haven't changed enough.

When daughter Linda had children, true to our word, she had a daughter just like her. As a child, Linda had more than her share of problems, in spite of my threats to end her earthly existence. Finding a place to sleep in her bed was one. It became a haven for every stuffed toy she could wheedle out of the family. Over time, there were enough of the fluffy beasts to occupy four-fifths of her bed, leaving the last fifth for her. Her own daughter's bed looks exactly the same.

The *hands off* rule was in full effect for both of them when shopping in stores. The mantra became, "Hold your thumbs behind your back." Sounds easy, doesn't it? But the power of the child to enjoy the *forbidden touch* comes to mind from a most delightful memory:

The Art of Grandparenting

One day, in Frank's Department Store, while shopping for clothing, both Rita and I noticed that daughter Linda had vanished. We did a quick aisle search. Nothing. Widening the search, we found her two aisles over at the end of a long row of stuffed animals. Bless her exploratory heart, with her thumb held tightly behind her back, obeying our directive, she walked past every animal on display, gently rubbing her nose on each one. She was one determined kid. Grand daughter Laura follows in her mother's footsteps, and we, Rita and I, know exactly where to follow her route whenever in a store.

And about that idea that you can 'give them back?' Never in a million years will I want to give them back, not permanently, at least. Grandchildren come to us only on loan, and the only interest grandparents must pay for enjoying time with them is the fatigue that sets in after they've returned home.

the Art of Grandparenting

Tips & Tricks

Even when a grandchild is destined to pass early, find the joyful moment in each day, and bring the child's laughter to life.

Watch your language around your grandchildren. They will most certainly repeat whatever you say, sometimes in a cheery, childish song.

Let the stuffed animals pile high in the child's bed. They represent safety in the dark of the night.

Children are resourceful; so much so that they will find ways to obey you and not obey you at the same time. Delight in their creativity!

Like mother, like daughter. Like father, like son. If you saw a quirky characteristic in your child, it may very well show up in your grandchildren. Be glad for the prior knowledge only you can have.

A Balancing Act of Love

Victoria Zackheim

IT'S SO EASY TO WRITE A PIECE about the joys of grandparenting. How the birth of a grandchild gives one a sense of continuity, that comforting sensation that the generations are moving forward toward some far-off time we'll never see, perhaps could never imagine, but there is progression nevertheless and we are but one small link in the endless family chain. For me, this impression that a part of my great-grandparents, my parents, and now me live on through my grandchildren is indeed comforting. And yet that knowledge, that continuation, pales next to the simple thrill of gathering my granddaughters into my arms—twin girls, nearly seven, so loving and smart, sweet and funny that their existence fills my heart, whether they are by my side or tucked into their beds fifteen miles away.

To understand my devotion, you must know these girls. They are compassionate—no teasing or bullying when they are around—and inquisitive. It is not enough to be raining, with a breathtaking rainbow that we must stop to appreciate, but I am expected to know *why* there are so many colors and *how* the arc is formed. They love

The Art of Grandparenting

to draw and write fairy tales, and they are readers! In fact, they have established their own reading corners in my home, where they snuggle in with books, assorted business cards and Post-its marking the chapters, and they become lost in their own unique and private worlds of imagination and delight.

My children were placed on this earth to be parents. Loving adults who married equally loving spouses. While my newlywed son and his wife have not yet started their family, my daughter and her husband have blessed us with these two girls. I have come to see that so much about my granddaughters that is loving, confident, and compassionate comes from these attentive and devoted parents, two people who encourage their children not to be alike—as so many parents do with twins—but to be who they are. The greatest compliment I can give them is that more children would grow into healthy adults, if only they could have parents like these.

I'm also happy to reveal that my daughter and her husband are very good at sharing. In fact, almost any time I'm available to pick up the girls at school or have them for an overnight, they are willing. I say "willing" because, unlike many parents, they don't relish shoving the girls out the door. In truth, their little family is perfectly happy to hang out together, hike in the nearby foothills, bike to the beach only minutes away, play games and, when the mood hits them, turn on the music and have a dance-a-thon that sometimes goes on long after bedtime. Nevertheless, I spend a significant amount of time with these two children who call me Mima, and I know with an unshakeable certainty that unless lightning strikes or the gods revolt, unless the world comes to an end or some major personality disorder suddenly becomes evident on my part, these girls will never be withheld from me. The door to their lives will never close and the

The Art of Grandparenting

visits will never stop. I know this because such cruelty is beyond the capacity of their parents. And yes, I am soothed by this knowledge, in heart and in mind.

But if this is so—if all is so ideal—you might be asking why I am writing about the fear of having a barrier built between these children and me?

The answer is simple: I know intellectually that this *withholding* will never happen, but I also understand that happen it does. In fact, it has been the heartbreak for several friends who, because of what in most cases was an arbitrary decision, were left bereaved and empty, banned from seeing their grandchildren, and left to struggle with a loss both unimaginable and devastating. A falling out with an adult child and the door is closed. A cross word to a daughter-in-law and that door is locked. A divorce where the child goes with the parent who is not the grandmother's child and that door becomes slammed and locked, with a deadbolt and security system added. One friend hasn't seen her daughter for nearly five years, nor has she ever seen her toddler grandchildren. Imagine knowing that you could walk past your grandchildren on the street and have no way to recognize them.

A dear friend's son came home one evening to find his wife and child gone. She had packed and returned to her parents' home with her two-month-old daughter. Days later, she announced that she was severing all ties with his family and they would never again see their only grandchild. My friend aged ten years in a matter of weeks, her despair made worse by the knowledge that no cross word had been spoken, no *evil mother-in-law* act committed. A case of post-partum depression that spun out of control...and everyone suffered.

There are times, of course, when grandparents are cut off from their children and grandchildren for a reason. Alcohol and drug

The Art of Grandparenting

abuse, religious fanaticism (one can be cut off for being a fanatic...or for not being one!). I was introduced to a woman who lives on the opposite side of the country from her son. She complained to me that her son and his wife were cruel and uncaring, but I know this woman to be very critical, always with an opinion that absolutely must be expressed. I imagine that her son and daughter-in-law finally drew the line, announcing that she was no longer welcomed in their home. Each year she receives one school picture and lives with the hollow space carved into her soul by her own sharp-tongued recalcitrance... which she fails to recognize.

It is human nature to fear losing that which is most precious to us. The perfect partner, the youthful body, the ideal job, the beloved pet. I rarely have nightmares about loss, but when I do it is nearly always about an accident befalling one of the girls. A car wreck, a kidnapping, some injury I can't prevent, no matter how desperately I try. If the injury is serious, the nightmare will move with me through my waking hours. I have learned that when these bad thoughts begin, it is best to shake myself awake and walk around, perhaps go downstairs and prepare a large mug of tea. Or read for a few hours, turn on the computer and work, anything to break this late-night theater of terror and helplessness.

When I became conscious of this fear—that of being shut off from the girls—I began to question my grandmother friends and was surprised to discover that nearly every one of them carried that same fear. For most of them, as for me, it is without basis: we have good, if not excellent, relationships with our adult children. And yet there we are, Baby Boomers sometimes reluctant to even admit much less share this fear that strikes in such a deep and vulnerable place. I asked a 'take no prisoners' friend if she ever worried about being alienated from her grandchildren, and her response was immediate. "My daughter-in-law threatened that once," she told me. "I looked her hard in the eye and told her, 'Those children will suffer terribly without me in their lives.' The threat was never carried out, nor was it ever repeated." Another friend had a different take. "I have one child and one grandchild; it's a very small circle. I've never imagined that my son would keep me from my grandson. But to be honest, I have no sense of generational pride. It has nothing to do with the fact that my grandson has my DNA, only that I see in him the boy my son once was, and my wish is very strong to make right whatever was wrong when I was young and he was young."

How do other cultures view this concern? I asked a friend in Paris, a woman with two daughters and three small grandchildren. While it is true that our worlds are not so very different, I learned long ago that the French—like the Japanese, Germans, Brazilians, Russians, etc.—have embedded in their cultures specific ideas about childrearing and grandparenting. When my friend responded, I found her observations poignant. "When I received your message, I thought smugly that this could never happen to me: my daughters need my baby-sitting, the little ones adore me, and my relationship with their parents is excellent. On further reflection, however, it's obvious that the relationship between grandchildren and grandparents, certainly until the grandchildren are old enough to be autonomous, is totally parent-dependent. I find myself being very careful about how I manage seeing my grandchildren, the time I spend with them, and how I take care of them. Although I do not think in terms of actually being *deprived* of them, I certainly *do* think in terms of ensuring that there is no ripple in how all this is handled—not always easy, but to me an essential component in my relationship with everyone concerned. I also want to say that, as I am sure you know, grandchildren are an extraordinary weapon. My son-in-law was married before and his ex-wife has made quite sure that his daughters will never see their paternal grandparents again."

Perhaps that is what I've been moving toward in this essay: the realization that children are a potent weapon that can be wielded by parents (and even grandparents) desiring to hold the power in the relationship. I've seen it happen—I'm quite sure that you have as well—and it's an ugly situation, this act of using children to gain power, or to assert control...or to simply be in charge.

Have you ever asked yourself what you could possibly do or say that would be so terrible as to push your own children over that line from *take the children whenever you like* to *they will no longer be spending time with you*? Would it be something as insignificant as a mild criticism levied against the child, or a suggestion to your child about parenting that is misconstrued as a condemnation? How fragile that relationship is between parent and adult child, especially if some of those relationship issues from your child's younger years were never successfully resolved. I was a loving mother to my young children, but with my grandchildren I am far more accepting, less likely to be critical of little things that seemed so big when I was struggling to be the perfect mother.

Grandchildren give us the opportunity to do it again...and do it right.

I'd like to exercise a little poetic license here and relate what I consider to be the ultimate grandmother story. When I was married, my husband's paternal grandparents ruled the roost as the undisputed heads of a large family. They were the founders of a business that grew under their guidance and provided very affluent lifestyles to perhaps a dozen people. It was July 4th and we had congregated at their son's home for his birthday celebration. Evening came and the intense heat had hardly abated. This son's daughter, who was also the youngest granddaughter, suggested that all of the grandchildren strip down and jump into the pool. Soon after the challenge, she and her husband did exactly that. In the water, they taunted the others to follow and, within minutes, my husband and I were treading water, quickly joined by my sister-in-law and her husband. So there we were, six young adults playing volleyball in the nude, our bodies illuminated to a ghastly blue-green by the eerie in-pool lighting. Suddenly, the elderly grandparents emerged from the house. The old man watched for a moment and then said, "Is it possible that they're all naked?" His wife glanced at her grandchildren and their spouses, turned to her octogenarian husband and with a shrug announced, "These are our grandchildren. If they're naked, it must be okay."

And that's what grandparenting is about: having the opportunity to love unconditionally, be playful and sometimes teach, revel in the joys of these children, and hopefully live long enough to see the adults they will become…and never be guided nor deterred by the fear that they could one day be taken away, leaving us with a gap in our hearts so large that winds could blow through and leave us without hope.

The Art of Grandparenting

Tips & Tricks

Fear of losing contact with grandchildren can be a good motivator for thinking before you leap in most situations.

Post-partum depression can cause the new mother to act irrationally. Get help for her and the whole family if necessary.

Be a grandparent whose vices are small and do not create big reasons for being cut off from the grandchildren.

Your natural urge to accept the whims of the grandchild needs to be blended liberally with an absence of criticism levied toward the child or his parents' ways of parenting.

Grandchildren need never to be used as weapons in the angry war games of adults.

When the grown grandchildren are swimming in the nude, you, in your infinite wisdom, will probably think that's perfectly all right.

Love unconditionally, and try to revel in the joys grandchildren have for life. They will bring delight to your life, too.

The Dirt Floor Visit
A Grandpa's Recollection

Hal Alpiar

"**O**hhhhh, G r a n p a !" The twelve-year-old actress's best melodramatic tone hangs pleadingly like a pregnant rain cloud. It borders carefully on the edge of reason because she knows he doesn't like whiners.

The sincerity of her tear-streaked upturned cheeks twinkles through the rising dull gray clutter around them in the room.

"I just don't understand," she snivels. "Every time I come here, I think the same thing, Granpa, and you know you don't make it easy either."

She gestures out the window that they face to indicate the early morning drizzle and smog-smothered rusted schoolbus twenty feet beyond. Minus an engine, the massive frame, still showing some signs of yellow is all but crushed, the tires flat and mangled, and just a smattering of shards remain in what were once the windows. Not knowing better, one might think the whole rear end had succumbed to a hand grenade attack and then left to massive corrosion while protecting thirty some odd years of burrows, lairs, and bird nests. Ivy strangles every protuberance; wild shrubs and tree limbs grow right up and tangle their way through the array of openings.

The Art of Grandparenting

"Why do you want to live here *any*way, Granpa? I mean *HERE?*" she asks, wincing with her last word. The innocence of her cherubic face is marred with wrinkled brow beyond her years.

He tilts his head ever so slightly back to the left and draws a deep breath. The word, "Shoooot!" with a slight Southern accent surfs softly under the curl of his upper lip on the exhale. She reminds him so much of her mother when she was that age... the same puzzled, pouting lines that sprout across her face. She is truly his daughter's daughter. How well he knew the signature theme of her stage presence training—projecting authenticity—was coming close to sucking him into her mother's theatrical vacuum of compliance, and her mother's growing need to produce and direct controlling influences on his life.

He tries to change the subject with a forced smile and empty questions about the classes she's taking at school (algebra already?), what her teachers are like, if she's found a boyfriend yet, what she's been doing on the weekends, whether she's still ice-skating.

He picks unobtrusively at a flake of tobacco stuck behind a front tooth. She's still staring blankly through the trailer window. With a folded napkin, he stretches to reach across his kitchen counter for a still-warm chocolate chip cookie, and hands it to her. He gets a half smile in return.

She takes the cookie and nibbles, but pretends not to notice his feigned exasperation or hear his small-talk questions. She turns now to look him full in the face (his whiskers look whiter now than she remembers) and prepares to continue with the speech she knew she'd end up having to deliver. It was after all what she wanted. It was her mother's quest.

Before her designer sneakers ever even crunched the gravel in his driveway, she knew what she needed to say. Her mother's failure to communicate with her own father had fallen to her. She had to be more than just a messenger; it was now her job to wrangle him in, get him to look again at his circumstances, re-consider the sense of it all. Somehow, she thought, without ever touching on the subject, she needed him to see that his age was getting to be an issue. He would surely rebel at any such reference, and then her whole cause would be lost.

The funny thing was that he probably knew why she was here, probably knew when her mother called to say she was on her way over. In fact, that's probably when he whipped up the cookie mix and stuck a tray full in the oven. It was stranger still to her that she knew how he'd react even before she turned the doorknob and called inside to him. So now, here she is with him—stage center—in the spotlight, a hushed audience. Of course no one was actually there except the two of them, but she was smart enough to realize that this scene would be recounted—maybe even re-performed—over the years and she wanted to have it end in her favor.

She wishes she could just take a bow, let the curtain drop, and change the topic. But she knows she needs to give a dazzling performance. She hates the idea of having to con him like this but it is, after all, for his own good. She lingers with the thought that they have such good talks and fun times when there's no agenda. But she stays on the message she's there to deliver.

"It's, it's just that you're *alone*, Granpa! Even when it's not drizzling like this, even when it's beautiful weather, this place is in the middle of...rustybusville, nowheresville...like, *nowhere!*" ("...*in this crummy, damp, dark, freezing cold, dirt floor trailer,*" she rehearsed saying, but didn't have the heart to add). "You know what I mean?" she added as if to punctuate her assessment.

Fingers a-splay, his palms turn slightly in and upwards. He shrugs a hapless, c'est la vie look. A small cough tumbles out as he twists his mouth to the right. He drops his hands and straightens

THE ART OF GRANDPARENTING

his shoulders. He metronomes his neck to the left and then to the right, and back again until it cracks. He breathes in deeply through his nose, raised ever so slightly as if to lift himself above the fray, and steps quietly toward her.

He thinks about the Ford place down the road where they "pulled out all the stops" on that new Explorer Sport truck that he really wanted, used to dream about. And the deal was almost made just because the sales guy was so nice, but no, he just wasn't ready to afford the thing, and had to fight back his emotions with rational logic, a decision reduced to the reality of what was affordable.

Her face comes up to his chest. She moves the cookie to her other hand and threads a now-freed finger through the side belt loop of his jeans, then pulls herself toward him. She sniffles. He gently strokes away the wrinkles on her forehead, and slides the back of his hand down her cheek to catch a tear. As if to signal his urge to withdraw, he slides both hands into his pockets, leaving his thumbs extended.

"You know you could…" she pauses; there's a hitch in her voice. She licks at the chocolate smudges in her palm. "You could, like, just stay with me and Mom? Granpa, you could…"

She sees from the reticence of his eyes that he's yet to buy in to her proposal. She's seen that look before. She knows he's hard to change his ways. She looks to the ceiling for inspiration… rain-stained tiles: reinforcement for the case she's trying to make, but no great convincing set of words lands on her shoulders. Tears well up. Her soft, lispy, high-pitched purring pleads the question. She does her best to paint the picture for him.

"You could, like, have *the w-h-o-l-e second floor!*" she says, sweeping the hand that holds two-thirds of the cookie toward his front door. A small crumb drops; she stoops to pick it up. Her gesture seems to suggest there would be lots more space for him to tinker in.

The Art of Grandparenting

She whisks her long strawberry blond hair back over her forehead, exposing her eyebrows, whose arcs now exude expectation. Pinches of stray blonde strands stay plastered to her glistening cheeks.

He's no longer sure of what he should be saying or doing, but falls back to the solution he's advanced so many times in the past, that some form of physical intimacy would somehow make everything all right. He starts to reach for her shoulder, but stops halfway and brings his hand—which appears to be acting on its own—instead, to his face where it strokes his beard.

Suddenly then, he fists-up his hand to cover his mouth as he lets out a string of swallowed, muffled body-shaking coughs timed as they were as if to syncopate her begging offer.

He starts to drop his hand to reach again for her, but finds himself forced to lean forward for one final cough. He looks down into the murky dark space near his boots, then grimaces. His still partly outstretched hand finally does find her shoulder. And finally too, he finds his craggy voice. He starts to speak. The word "Listen" sandwiches another cough and comes out as three syllables.

"Granpa, are you okay?"

Moving slowly, almost gingerly, he straightens up, clears his throat, forces a smile, and answers her.

"Listen, Honey," his voice raspy, but he speaks sweetly and consolingly, "you tell your mother that ah truly do 'ppreciate the second floor, but tell her that I reckon too many of mah years *already* been…well, *up in the air!*"

He pauses to see if he can tell whether she understands. She stares at him vacantly.

"Y'all know what I mean, Sweetheart? It's a great thing that you both think of me like that, but, well, second floor…I just…er, heights…heights make me a little dizzy an' all, y'know? Ever since

The Art of Grandparenting

that day that fire department truck got me offa that roof with that puppy I raced back inside for..." He trails off.

He pats her twice on the neck like she was Clementine, the sheepdog from up the hill, then drops his arm and turns away. She takes his hand and locks her fingers with his. Her palm is soft, cold and clammy; his feels calloused, warm and dry.

He spits off to the side—"*Hagggggght-TU!*"—and swipes his sleeve across his mouth. The racking coughs start again. She squeezes his hand as if the pressure alone might relieve him. It takes him a few minutes for the wheezing and hacking to subside. He mumbles some apology to her. Her face is twisted with worry.

"Listen, Sweetie, I know it must seem hard for you and your mom to understand, but..." he spits again..."you tell 'er, your mother, that I said thank you very much, an' that I love you both with my whole heart and soul, but that mah dirt here works *jus'* fine for me."

Still clutching his fingers, she circles around to face him.

"*Ohhhh, Granpa!*" Her sad face bumps his chest affectionately. She swipes her wet eyes against his heavy plaid shirt and hugs his arm, which vibrates in concert with the tiny nervous twitch under his left cheekbone.

They stand that way for two or three long searching minutes. Her faster pulse, his slower, seem to trade places now through their fingertips. She wonders what her mother will say now, now that she realizes she'll have to report back to her that he's just not going to budge. Oh, how much of her mother she sees in him... the stoicism, the stubbornness, the misplaced sense of pride and independence. Like being hit with a big ocean wave at the beach, there comes a point you simply need to give in and scramble back to the sand, which even in all its shiftiness offers relative stability.

"I guess you're right, Granpa," she finally breaks the silence.

The corners of her mouth turn up ever so slightly. A dimple breaks the surface. He looks unsure of what it is that she thinks he's right about.

"Mom definitely wouldn't like you spitting on the floor, even if it *was* the *second* floor." A smile inches across his face; it gains momentum as it draws in the corners of his eyes.

She looks up at him and grins. His cheeks rise to push his eyes into a squint. He chuckles and kisses her forehead tenderly, then walks her slowly to the door.

Like pulling magnets apart, their fingertips finally separate. She opens the door and steps down, then heads up the driveway rattling the gravel, still nibbling the cookie. She stops abruptly and heads over to the old schoolbus, snaps three branches of wild lilac from where there had once been a right front fender, clutches them together and walks back to hand them to him in a dazzling array of purple and white perfume. She smiles and heads off once more, turning back twice to wave, then throws him a kiss before disappearing into the fog.

Lilacs in hand, he leans to the doorframe and lingers there a moment longer, then—eyes to the floor—closes the door and returns inside. He sniffs at the flowers and leans the branches into his kitchen sink where he covers the drain and runs a small puddle of water. He wonders why he never thought about bringing lilacs inside. The fragrance is intoxicating. He returns to his room looking for any sign of her footprints among the scrambled marks of his boot treads.

There's nothing there.

"*Second floor?*" he says to himself. "Ah ain't even figured out what to do with this here *first* floor besides weed it, spit on it, and dig it for fishin' worms. Hmmph!"

He turns to the sink. "Damn, those flowers sure do smell like somethin' special!"

He wanders over to look out the window. "Now did ah jus' have this here conversation with her or am I dreamin' it?" He gives his eyes

The Art of Grandparenting

a wake-up rub. He sees the plateful of cookies, but can't remember if he made eleven or twelve. Shaking his head, he picks one up and bites into it, chews and swallows, then takes a deep, breath. Lilac fills him.

He remembers racing frantically across parts of four states in the middle of the night to get to his daughter's side within an hour of this favorite child's birth, this first grandchild. He hadn't expected to leave so abruptly and was in such a dither couldn't find the gifts he wanted to bring.

He grabbed a baseball as he rushed out through his garage, and wrote some loving autograph on it at the first stoplight that held him captive at a busy intersection.

He finishes the cookie, and gazes now hard into the thickening fog that rolls past his window. He scratches his head.

He remembers feeling so excited at seeing and lifting and cuddling this tiny creature that there wasn't even any room for feeling stupid about the baseball until days later and, by then, his daughter was actually bragging about the creativity of his thoughtfulness. What a blessing that daughter, and now this baseball-loving (of course!) granddaughter who comes to him out of the fog on a mission to move him in with her and her mom.

"One thing's for damn sure though, ah must say, that there child—she surely is a chip off mah daughter's block. *Spittin' on the second floor*...ha, ha, ha, ha, ha, ha, ha, ha!"

His laughter fills the trailer. And real or dreamt just plain doesn't matter because—like the thoughts of every grandfather's granddaughter—her visit has filled his heart.

the Art of Grandparenting

Tips & Tricks

Bake cookies as soon as you know they are coming to visit you.

Listen to your grandchildren.

Smell the lilacs.

Remember, no matter what your circumstance, your grandchildren love you.

I Like Grandpa

Gene Matthews

Sarah must have been around six months old when she first spoke to me. Interestingly, I was the only one who understood her. She was lying on her back in her crib, gurgling and cooing when I bent over and said "Sarah, say 'I like Grandpa.'"

Instantly, she broke into a delightful grin and screamed, "Eeaahh iiee annno."

"She said it," I cried. "Sarah said 'I like Grandpa.'"

Sarah's parents came running into the room with the most doubtful of expressions on their faces.

"Watch this," I said. Again I bent over the crib, looked Sarah in the eyes and said "Sarah, say 'I like Grandpa.'"

"Eeahh iiee annno" she shrieked in response.

"There. See. She said it. She said it," I yelled as I began to dance around the room.

My son and daughter-in-law looked at me with mingled expressions of pity and concern but I knew that my first grandchild had proclaimed to the world that she liked me. This had been my first encounter with her because my wife and I served overseas as

THE ART OF GRANDPARENTING

missionaries in Korea and only occasionally made it back to America for home visits.

Next month Sarah graduates from college with a degree in performing arts. She has already begun auditioning for movies and singing gigs and has starred in various musicals already in her young life and she still likes me.

Grandchildren are supposed to love their grandparents. It's part of the package. Somewhere it is writ large that grandchildren shall love those decrepit old people no matter how seldom they see them, how weird they appear, how strange they smell, or how funny they talk. This edict is usually enforced by mom and dad to the extent that the grandchildren become terrified lest they slip up and fail to love the old geezers properly.

That's why a grandchild who sincerely likes his or her grandparents is such a delight.

Several years passed and Sarah had a sister named Jillian. Several more years passed and Sarah and Jillian both moved to Korea where their parents had jobs teaching in a school where English was the language of instruction.

Jillian liked me too. I sensed that the first time I saw her in the Atlanta airport during our first visit home after she was born. Her mother carried her out to the baggage claim area to meet us and as soon as she saw me, Jillian reached out to allow me to take her in my arms. Her mother was astounded. She explained that Jillian had never warmed up to strangers. I pointed out that I was not a stranger because I was a grandpa.

Shortly after they moved to Korea, our door bell rang quite late at night. When we opened the door Jillian was there with her parents. She was wearing a bloody shirt and had a neat row of stitches in her forehead and was carrying a sack of doughnuts. Dad and mom explained that, while playing on the swings with her friends, she

The Art of Grandparenting

had fallen and bashed her head. She had agreed to go have her head stitched back together only if dad and mom promised to take her to get some doughnuts and go see grandpa.

It turns out Jillian was a chronic basher. The above scenario was repeated often enough that when the doorbell rang at night we were pretty certain Jillian had inflicted another gash on some part of her anatomy. Her parents even began to wonder if the frequency of occurrence might stem at least in part from a combined love of donuts and a strong liking for Grandpa. Jillian is now in college where she plays soccer on the varsity team. She still bashes herself occasionally, and she still likes me.

But it came to pass that our daughter got married and before long there were three more grandchildren. Dylan was a little shy around me at first because again he heard about me before we met. Liking a grandpa who lives halfway around the world is hard, but we soon became acquainted during a home visit, and after moving back to Iowa we spent more time with him and soon learned how delightfully manipulative he could be. He was highly intelligent. I can brag about this because he bears none of my genes. We adopted his mother in Korea when she was three.

After retirement, we moved back to Iowa City, a fairly short distance from where Dylan lived with his parents. It was close enough that he could occasionally spend a night with us. "Grandpa," he said on one such occasion. "When we go out for ice cream after supper, can we drive around and look at the Christmas decorations."

Both Dylan's Grandma and I were unaware until that moment that we were going out for ice cream but we quickly agreed that driving around to look at the Christmas decorations after having ice cream would be a good idea.

When Alysia was born she looked more like her mother than her mother did. That probably does not make sense but is,

The Art of Grandparenting

nevertheless, true. She has dimples and they drive me wild. Early on, she also displayed a trait that I now realize is fairly common with grandchildren who like their grandparents. She liked to climb on my lap whenever I sat down in her vicinity. She discovered that if I blew my cheeks out, she could whomp them with her hands and make the air and whatever else was in there blow out all over her. She could keep this up for long stretches of time and it was always accompanied by lots of giggling and cries for more. She also developed a fondness for head butting. This occurred by accident the first time when she became too enthusiastic about the cheek-whomping, but she enjoyed it so much, it soon was worked into the routine. I came away from each encounter with flaming cheeks and a bruised forehead. Alysia left each time all giggly and hyped and badly needing the ride home as a chance to calm down enough to go to bed. And both of us parted with renewed assurance that we liked each other.

Deryck was the last to appear and his name verified his parents' fondness for the letter "y." We made it to the hospital shortly after his birth and he looked quite capable of filling in as linebacker in the future. He grew and developed quickly, displaying physical sturdiness and a fondness for things mechanical. He soon amassed a remarkable collection of toy cars, tractors, trucks, and tools, along with books about cars, tractors, trucks and tools. He began to compete a bit with Alysia for the right to climb in my lap, whomp my cheeks and butt heads but his forays were always accompanied by a large collection of cars, trucks, tractors, and tools and, of course, books about same. Running toy trucks across bald heads is not very comfortable but is usually tolerated because the activity was certain testimony that Deryck liked me.

But gradually, THE PROBLEM became apparent. Deryck could not talk. He tried. Garbled sounds emerged from his mouth and it was obvious that he was trying to say something but the sounds were undecipherable. His speech soon became a strange mixture of groans, grunts and squeals.

He underwent batteries of tests. The medical tests all revealed him to be a very healthy young boy. His hearing was excellent. Physically, he was normal in every way.

A speech therapist then had a go at him and her diagnosis was grim. Deryck had a rare condition consisting of some sort of disconnect between his brain and his tongue. His brain was normal but the wiring was broken somehow. Her prognosis was that Deryck would probably never be able to speak properly and his parents were advised to find a way to teach him sign language.

Lessons were begun and Deryck picked up sign language quickly. He even began to teach it to his older brother and sister.

I was taken aback one day when visiting shortly after the family had moved into a new home Deryck's father had just built. We were moving from room to room of the spacious home when Deryck suddenly grabbed my hand, pulled me aside and in a perfectly articulated voice said, "Grandpa, do you want to see my room?"

In a final act of desperation, Deryck's parents took him to still another specialist who put him through a great battery of tests, all of which he passed with flying colors. Her conclusion was that Deryck was highly intelligent and somewhat competitive. He had experienced frustration at being unable to keep up with his older siblings and had invented a way to force them to rely on him by learning "his" language. At the age of nine he speaks normally, loves feeding the goats on his parent's farm and occasionally writes songs which his older brother puts to music. The last time I saw him he gave me a hug, and I felt strong confirmation that he likes me.

A major problem with grandchildren is that they grow up. Head butting and cheek whomping and lap climbing and horsing around in general are inevitably deemed too undignified for teen-agers and

The Art of Grandparenting

young adults. They still like me and I am fiercely proud of them but a part of the joy disappears as they grow up. Grandparents tend to move in the opposite direction. As they age they become sillier and begin to yearn for somebody with whom to share the silliness. A major privilege of grandparenting is to turn the grandchildren on, get them hyped up then turn them back to their parents. This only works with little children.

I have discovered, however, that there is an endless supply of grandchildren if we only look for them. It began innocently enough in church one Sunday when I noticed a shy little boy who had either had a bad experience or had not slept well the night before. Without thinking, I walked up to him, stuck out my hand, palm up and said, "Give me five." His face lit up with a smile and he cheerfully slapped my hand. Before long every child in church was seeking me out to "give me five" after each service.

The practice soon spread to the children in the pre-school and day care center that meets in our church. If I happen to be in the church on week-days I visit each room where the children of various ages spend their days. As I enter each room, all activity stops as the children come running with cries of "I want five!" followed by hand slaps from each. Some even insist on "giving me ten" by slapping both hands at the same time. A couple of the stronger boys vie with each other to see who can cause the most damage to Grandpa's poor hand.

A few weeks ago I had a meeting at the church in the morning as some of the children were arriving with their parents. One little boy saw me, tugged his mother's hand to attract attention, pointed at me and cried out, "He's a grandpa. We like him!"

It's a good thing they do because I like them too.

The Art of Grandparenting

Tips & Tricks

When your grandchild says something only you can understand such as, "Eeaahh iiee annno," and you know it means, "I like Grandpa," let the parents pity you, or tease you, or worry about you. You know the truth!

Develop a "Grandpa Game" that can become a routine way to play with your grandchildren. If cheek whomping and head butts are not your style, find something fun that is. Simple finger-magic games, or counting toes, or making goofy faces come to mind.

As your grandchildren grow up to be teens and young adults, long outgrowing the silliness of childhood, and as you become sillier and sillier in your old age, there may other little kids in your realm who might see you as a surrogate grandpa. Use the *high five* hand greeting to start the ball rolling with a host of new "grandchildren" who will see you and say, "He's a grandpa. We like him!"

EPILOGUE
Becoming Grammie

Valerie Connelly

The long drive to Nashville began at 4 AM and ended at 1:15 PM. As my daughter, Liz and her husband, Todd were just backing out of their garage to take little Charlie to his first check up, I pulled my car around the cul-de-sac, screeched to a halt in front of their house, hopped out of the car—as best one can hop after sitting behind the wheel for just over nine hours with only two rest stops—and ran to the car's right side, back seat window to see my first grandbaby in the flesh. His little body, his tiny fingers, the peace reflected in his serene face, and the first touch of my hand to his velvety cheek, all conspired to overwhelm my usual reserve. Tears of joy just burst from my eyes in an unbidden deluge of long-pent-up emotion.

"Hi Mom!" my daughter said, laughing at me in a loving way.

"Sorry we have to go right now," my son-in-law said, leaning toward me across the divide between the front seats. "The pediatrician is forty-five minutes away. Gotta go!"

"I'll probably just take a nap till you guys get back, okay?" I gulped back the lump choking me, and swiped at my eyes to brush

The Art of Grandparenting

away the evidence of my vulnerable state. I suddenly wasn't tired at all, in spite of the sleepless night and high-tension hours of waiting and worrying helplessly at long distance through Liz's twenty-nine-hour labor and delivery, the long drive from Wisconsin to Tennessee, and the nervous energy expended all along the way.

"That's fine. Remember to let the dogs out first and to turn off the alarm," Liz said.

"What's the code?" My brain just couldn't remember that valuable detail, which upon hearing it, I recognized instantly. As they drove away, I knew I was walking into one of the greatest adventures of my life—becoming Grammie.

As I opened the door into their home, the dogs greeted me with a barrage of yelps and woofs. I petted Daisy and Morris, who do no damage to furniture when home alone, and freed Ellie from her crate, confined there because she destroys things when unsupervised. All three escaped gladly into the backyard as I took a look around the open living spaces. This house needs some serious cleaning! My daughter's penchant for keeping things up had obviously dwindled away during the last couple of months. *I'll give them a real gift while they're gone for these couple of hours. I'll make this place sparkle!* My inner voices marched into battle. *You don't even clean your own house! Remember your back! Be careful!* I knew I could make a dent in the dust, dog hair dust bunnies, and clutter. I knew it wasn't beyond my physical limitations to take out the recycling that tumbled from under the sink when I opened the cabinet door. I could push a vacuum, wield a Swiffer, and swipe a mop with the best of them. *You know this is gonna hurt later on!* Negative thoughts be damned! *Who cares?* And I went to work.

There is something cathartic about housework when done as a gift to people you love. I surprised myself with the vigor I brought to the tasks that, at least on the surface, made the place look clean.

THE ART OF GRANDPARENTING

I skipped the stairs and didn't drag the heavy vacuum upstairs. But I did the dishes, polished the kitchen counters, wiped away the weeks of neglect from all visible surfaces like there was no tomorrow, leaving the urge to really scrub the floor and clean out the fridge for another day. I even dragged my luggage upstairs to the bonus-room-turned-Grammie-hideaway, where I would sleep under the ceiling fan amidst the jumbled books, CDs, boxed-up memories, stowed exercise equipment and stashed furniture. I carved out a spot for my laptop on the surface of the desk Liz and I had once procured from a garage sale and quickly made up the bed.

The dogs' barking and the rumble of the garage door alerted me that I had finished just in time. A little sweaty from my work, I skipped down the stairs and waited for them to come through the door.

"Hi, Mom!" Liz was beaming as Todd carried the car seat and its precious cargo into the living room. He lifted little Charlie from the tangle of straps, adjusted the swaddling blanket a little bit and held him toward me.

"Oh! He's so beautiful!" was all I could stammer as little Charlie snuggled into my arms, somehow knowing this was a safe place to be. "Oh, so beautiful!"

There is no other moment in life to match holding the first grandchild for the first time. And to think! Over the next two weeks, this experience would initiate me into the club of first-time grandparents. I got to relish the time cradling this baby in my arms for hours as his parents tried to catch up on their sleep by cat-napping. I would become the world's iPhone camera photo-snapping expert, able to capture in digital clarity—with one hand, yet!—every nuance of my grandson's facial expressions as he slept.

I think one funny aspect of being a new grandparent is learning the new lingo that goes with all the new and incredible STUFF

THE ART OF GRANDPARENTING

today's young parents have to make parenting easier and safer than ever. I had to keep myself from saying, "Wow! We didn't have *that* when you were a baby!" more than twice or three times a day. It is a whole new and very brave world for young parents and their kids.

My new lingo initiation started with learning that *Hypnobabies* was not meditation for newborns. It was the self-hypnosis method of pain reduction during labor—oops! I mean, *birthing*—which teaches the pregnant parents how to switch tension—and therefore pain—off as contractions—oops! I mean *pressure waves*—become more regular and more intense. The *doula*—midwife—participates during the training of the soon-to-be parents, and then is present throughout the birthing. She also follows up a week after delivery by coming to the home and interviewing the parents. I was pleased to be included in this, and I can say that, if I had had this option when I was a young mother, I'd have been an advocate for *hypnobabies* myself.

Next on my newbie grandparent syllabus was the terminology for some of the gizmos that make the parental task easier when attempting to calm babies.

"Hey, Mom, can you get me the *Boppie*?"

The first time Liz asked me this question, I stared at her like a zombie, totally befuddled and feeling very ignorant.

"Uh, the *Boppie*?"

"Yeah, that crescent-shaped pillow with all the zoo animals on it? I think it's on the table next to the sofa."

I walked into the living room, scanned the area, and came up with the *Boppie*, which really looks like a much larger version of the travel pillow one puts around one's neck in airplanes.

We used the *Pack n' Play* attachment for diaper changing, although a bonafide changing table waits up in the nursery. The *Pack n' Play* is the ultimate bassinette cum travel bed cum playpen. It can be used for many purposes and for now is acting as Charlie's

THE ART OF GRANDPARENTING

bassinette, snuggled next to Liz's side of the bed. Today's newborn Huggies are actually leak-proof, stretchy, with Velcro tabs, and come with a blue stripe down the front and back that turns green when the baby wets or deposits more in this, the twenty-first century disposable diaper. Parents don't have to sniff for poop, risk a getting a stinky, gooey finger when checking for poop, or worry about a baby-produced accident on some unsuspecting stranger's lap. These mini-miracles are a long way from those first disposable diapers that routinely gapped around the baby's leg allowing all manner of gooey stuff to emerge at the most inopportune moments, all held together with sticky, pull-away paper tabs that clung to the parent's fingers and would not let go, to make putting them on the baby all the more comical and difficult.

And of course, we had Desitin or Vaseline for diaper rash. Today's parents have *Beaudreaux's Butt Paste*, which magically eliminates rash in short order. And if the parents want to use cloth diapers, gone are the days of dangerous diaper pins, bulky, leaky rubber pants, and diaper pails that stink up the house enough to overpower the cat's litter box. Today there is a choice between *Bummi's Preferred Super Whisper Wraps*—machine washable cloth diapers with a moisture-proof cloth cover, and the *Bumgenius Reusable Diaper*, which is actually an all-in-one absorbent copy of the disposable diaper, but the inside part that gets messy is removable and therefore washable, and so is the cover itself. I never once used a cloth diaper on my kids. But in today's world, cloth diapers are as easy to use as disposables, and while they cost a pretty penny to begin with, over time, they are much cheaper than their land-fill-bound counterparts.

When it comes to breast-feeding, the ultimate maternal experience and best food for the baby, taking care of the breast itself is aided by *Mother Love Nipple Cream*, a healthy, ingestible concoction of coconut oil and olive oil. Of course, you should go to

THE ART OF GRANDPARENTING

your *Lactation Specialist,* for weekly meetings and get the answers on what you are doing right and what you can do better so nursing is most efficient and effective. The babies get weighed before and after feeding, so the mothers can know their milk is doing the job and is plentiful.

I had the pleasure of going to two such meetings with Liz, and I came to realize that not all mothers have an easy time breast-feeding. The lactation specialist—also a doula—was a wonderfully informative, chatty, personable woman with kids of her own, who put everyone at ease, used lots of praise, and sold swaddling blankets, baby wraps and breast pumps as well. Baby wraps are no longer modified packs, as the *Snugglie* was and still is. No, you have the *Maya Wrap,* and *The Ultimate Baby Wrap* among many others. These are six-foot long swaths of material wrapped around parent and child to engulf the child safely and hold the baby close, whether in front, on the side or in back, so the parents have hand-free capabilities from the beginning. These are great for shopping, doing things around the house, going for walks, and just being close.

But, to be discrete in today's PC world, the nursing mother absolutely must have the nursing cover called the *Hooter Hider* by some, and otherwise known as the *Bébé au Lait.* This is a wide swath of beautifully printed material which covers the baby and exposed breast by hanging from a wide band looping around the mother's neck and attached to a stiffened edge of the cloth. This allows the mother to see her baby, the baby to see its mother, and no one else to see what's going on back there in the circular booth of the local pizza place. Where is the adventure and excitement of nursing in an embarrassment-riddled world that thinks breast-feeding is an unseemly, primitive act? Oh, for the days of the frayed, flannel baby blanket that fell to the floor or blew off in the wind leaving the beauty of the act of nourishing a baby for all to see!

THE ART OF GRANDPARENTING

And for those times when you really have to put the baby down while awake and engaged in the world around him or her, we now have the *Newborn Soothing Center*. This is the techno-toy lover's ultimate electronic swing. It can be programmed to move as the parents do, back and forth or up and down at different speeds, and to produce a heart beat, a rolling surf, plain white noise, or even music from your iPOD synchronized to the rhythm of the plush-covered cocoon holding your baby safe and sound. There are dangling doo-jiggies to captivate the baby's attention, and basically, there is no reason for a child to feel abandoned to the swing. I'd wager kids who fit in these mini-environments love to be there!

Well, I must admit that, as my two weeks with Charlie and his parents were drawing to a close, I felt a wave of sadness that completely redefined how I look at the world. Grammie is not just a name. Grammie is a new lifestyle. Grandparenthood produces a new beginning in life that makes the last lap of the race more vibrant, more invigorating, ever more philosophical and in many ways more important than all that has gone before. I plan to make the most of my allotted time with Charlie and any other grandchildren who may come into my life.

As I drove away from their house, waving to my daughter who stood in the doorway, holding up Charlie's hand to wave back, I felt an overwhelming rush of emotion. It was all-powerful. I quickly understood that this grandparent's form of love made me more than reluctant to leave. I felt a strong unwillingness to be banished to some distant place, to allow any significant distance to come between me and them. It's not enough to say that I didn't want to leave them behind. I had no choice as I turned the corner but to pull over to the side of the street. Sobbing, gasping, letting the tears flow unchecked, I vowed to build all manner of bridges to the love this little baby and his parents released in me. I vowed to stay close, to be a meaningful contributor to Charlie's future. I suddenly realized that in these two weeks I had gained—forever—an incredible gift. This is my chance to live what I now know to be the ultimate honor in human experience. I get to join the legions of others who also find this time of life irrevocably infused with unquenchable joy. How is this possible? All this came to be simply by becoming Grammie.

ABOUT THE AUTHORS

WHEN THIS PROJECT BEGAN I wasn't in any way sure who would want to join with me in creating a book for new grandparents. I put out a call to authors I had interviewed on my radio program, CALLING ALL AUTHORS. I informed my grandparent-authors at Nightengale Press of the project. I mentioned it to colleagues and I put some information in a couple of popular writer's newsletters asking for published authors to contribute to this book. It is just astonishing to me what happens when a person simply puts the word out. Better than spreading bread upon the water and waiting for the ducks, or geese, or swans to gobble it up, asking authors to write about something so close to their lives and hearts is like pouring honey on an anthill. Those who came forward are all talented, helpful and honestly delightful people. This section provides a bit of information about them, see them each pictured with a grandchild or grandchildren, and I hope, will be the icing on an already decadently delicious cake. Do visit their websites, and go to www.theartofgrandparenting.com to join in the fun! Blog, share photos and videos, enter contests, learn tips and tricks, and connect with others who, like you, are learning The Art of Grandparenting.

—Valerie Connelly, Editor and Publisher

ROSE PADRICK

Born in inner city New York Rose moved at an early age to Florida. Rose and her husband still make their home very close to the neighborhood where they raised their five children. She draws upon her experiences as a mother and a grandmother as inspiration for her column 'Rose's Room' voted one of two most popular columns in the Florida Today newspaper. 'Roses Room' is now running in the Boca Raton newspaper and Brevard County Woman magazine. 'Rose's Corner' column ran for a year in Seniors Today magazine, and Rose does weekly threads for Brevard County Moms website.

Several of Rose's short stories have been published in Senior Life, The Best Of Times, Camping Today, Literary Liftoff—the official magazine of the Space Coast Writers Guild—Coastal Angler, and Quiltwork. She appeared in two double page spreads with pictures in the November 2006 and 2007 issues of Woman's World Magazine. Rose's yet-to-be published children's book ran for two years as monthly chapter features in the Pet Gazette magazine, and previously ran as a weekly cliffhanger in the Deland Beacon newspaper. She hopes to change Sparky's Adventures status from 'yet-to-be published' to 'recently published' very soon.

CAROLE BLAKE

Carole has been a song lyricist for over thirty years. Several of her songs—from Disco to Country to Children's songs—have been recorded and released on various record labels. One of them, "Kitchen Band", was purchased by and played on the Shari Lewis TV Show. She was also an executive producer of the motion picture "The Night The Lights Went Out In Georgia", starring Dennis Quaid.

Carole has written articles for several Long Island newspapers, including The Nassau Herald, The South Shore Record, and North Shore Today. She is currently the "humor writer" for a new magazine called "Peer Observations", which is all about health. The last piece she wrote for this magazine was called, "I'm Giving TiVo the Heave-ho!"

For the past decade Carole has been living with a wonderful man named Larry. She wrote an article entitled "What's-His-Name" about him and the dilemma as to what to call one's "boyfriend" when one is over fifty! This article was published in a Senior newspaper in the Midwest. She has a lovely daughter and a great son, and they are both married to terrific people. And...Carole has two fantastic grandsons (so far), Jake and Davis.

CAROL MULLER-FUNK

When Carol was in the fifth grade she had a poem published in the Wee Wisdom magazine. The writing bug struck and she has been writing ever since. It has been only recently after retirement from teaching that she began writing for publication. After losing her husband in 1999, she remarried, and in addition to a new husband she found herself an instant grandmother of eight adopted grandchildren, making, at present, a total of sixteen grandchildren—including her own) and one great-grandchild. Did she say "retired?"

"It has certainly been a new learning experience," she explains: "In my article Becoming a Grandmother Without Even Trying, I have attempted to pass on to others a bit of advice which I hope will be useful."

In 2005, Nightengale Press published her book, *Golden Love*, (ISBN 1-933449-20-9 $9.95), about how to remarry after sixty. It is available in the Store at www.nightengalepress.com and on all online bookstores.

BOB KASCHT

Bob Kascht was a retired physician who lived in Waukesha, Wisconsin with his wife, Mary Ann. For thirty years as a pathologist he studied and described diseases and tumors, and honed his powers of observation. His book, *Good Genes, Luck, Lots of Prayer*, was published in 2008 by Nightengale Press. (ISBN 1-933449-64-0 $15.95)

In the last twenty years he changed his focus, refined his vocabulary and expanded his interests to include documentation of human foibles and musings about the meaning of it all. He had a wide range of interests, especially the world of nature, the outdoors and concerns for ecology.

Sadly, Bob passed away suddenly in June 2009, shortly after submitting his essay for this anthology. I received a hand-written note and an article about grandparenting by Judith Viorst from him just a day or two after he died. Bob was a witty and earnst man and a pleasure to know.

IRENE WATSON

Irene Watson, author of award winning *The Sitting Swing: Finding Wisdom to Know the Difference* (Ann Arbor, Michigan: Loving Healing Press, 2009,) was born and raised in a tiny hamlet of Reno in the northern area of the province of Alberta in Canada. It was a farming community, mostly settled by immigrants from Russia, Ukraine and Poland during the early 1900s. She received her Master's Degree in Psychology, with honors, from Regis University, Denver. Irene and her husband, Robert, live in Austin, Texas. She is also author/editor of *The Story That Must be Told: True Tales of Transformation*, and, *Authors Access: 30 Success Secrets for Authors and Publishers* and is in the process of co-authoring another book, *Rewriting Life Scripts: Transformational Recovery for Families* which will be published in the Fall of 2009.

Irene is the president of Higher Power Foundation, Inc., and facilitator of transformative women's retreats and workshops. She brings forty years of life changing experiences, facilitation and study into her hands-on programs. She is also the Managing Editor of Readerviews a book review and author publicity service.

BARBARA ABERCROMBIE

Barbara Abercrombie has published books for children, novels for adults and essays that have appeared in the *LA Times, Baltimore Sun, Christian Science Monitor* and in the anthologies *For Keeps* and *The Face in the Mirror*. Her most recent books are: *Courage & Craft: Writing Your Life into Story* and a picture book for kids, *The Show & Tell Lion*. She teaches creative writing in the Writers' Program at UCLA Extension, conducts writing workshops for the Wellness Community and lives with her husband in Santa Monica, California and Twin Bridges, Montana. She writes an ongoing blog for writers: www.WritingTime.net .

HANNAH YAKIN

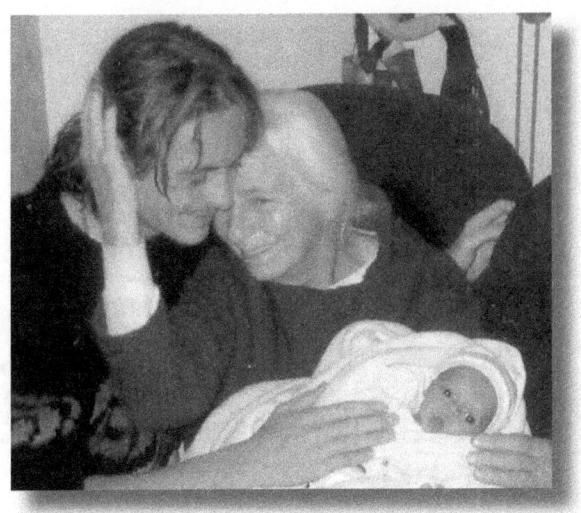

Born in Amsterdam, Hannah Yakin studied art in the Netherlands and Paris. She emigrated to Israel in 1956 and married Israeli artist Abraham Yakin in 1957. Together with her husband she has exhibited her art all over Israel, Europe and the United States. Living in Jerusalem, the couple has eight children, twenty-three grandchildren and a steadily growing number of great-grandchildren.

Hannah is the author of adult and children's fiction. The Dutch versions of her novels *Hier is je bruidegom* (Here is Your Bridegroom) and *Jardena, Dagboek uit Jeruzalem* (Jardena, a Jerusalem Diary) were published in Holland. Her short stories and articles have appeared in literary magazines in Holland, the United States and Israel. "The Gottlieb Menagerie," "The Land of Milk and Honey, Freckles and Wrinkles" were broadcast by the BBC. Her story, "Of Tortoises and Other Jews" became *Yan's Daughter*, a play by Patricia O'Donovan, regularly produced in Israel since 2004. Learn more at www.yakinart.com

JUDITH MAMMAY

Judith Mammay grew up in Vermont and earned her B.S. in Physical Education at the University of New Hampshire. She taught three years, and lived in New Hampshire with her husband for most of their married life. A stay-at-home mom until her youngest entered first grade, she then earned a Master's degree in Learning and Language Disabilities before going back to work as an exceptional education teacher at an inner city school. Judith taught students with a variety of disabilities for seventeen years, which served her well when one of her grandsons was diagnosed with autism.

Upon retirement, Judy moved to Florida to begin her second career as a children's book writer, producing two early readers—*It's Time* and *Ryan's Victory,* and a mid-grade book, *Knowing Joseph,* all about autism. She had articles published in *The Autism Perspective (TAP)*. She graduated from the Institute of Children's Literature. She is a member if the Space Coast Writers' Guild (SCWG) and the Society for Book Writers and Illustrators (SCBWI). Judy enjoys nature photography, playing golf, and spending time with her grandchildren. She sees her grandchildren regularly. Visit her website at www.judithmammay.com

ROCHELLE JEWEL SHAPIRO

Like the heroine of her novel, *Miriam the Medium,* (Simon & Schuster,) Rochelle is a phone psychic who lives in Great Neck, Long Island. She has written about her psychic work in *New York Times (Lives)* and *Newsweek, My Turn,* as well as having articles written about her in *Jewish Week, The Jerusalem Post,* and *Redbook Magazine.* Her novel is now selling in Holland, Belgium, the U.K. and in the U.S. Her poem, *Second Story Porch* has been nominated for a Pushcart Prize by *The Schuykill Valley Review.* She teaches writing at UCLA Extension and reviews books for *Kirkus, PW, JBooks,* and *Southern California Review.* And she adores her grandchildren. Now there are two—Jacen (two years old) as well as Rebecca who appears in this essay.

GERRI HELMS

Gerri Helms is a Life and Health Coach, working with people who wish to make lifestyle changes that are conducive to weight loss and maintenance. She also leads teleseminars and workshops and spiritual retreats geared toward the betterment of women. *Trust God and Buy Broccoli, a Spiritual Approach to Weight Loss* was published in 2007. In this book she shares with readers how she lost over 100 pounds and has kept it off for sixteen years with concepts that may help readers in situations where they may experience difficulties in sticking to their *diet*. Prior to coaching, Gerri spent twenty-five years in the corporate arena, and today she shares that business experience with clients. She has also written for the Brevard County Magazine and has been featured on many radio and internet blog shows. Visit www.lifecoachgerri.com for all the details.

DONNE DAVIS

Donne Davis spent fifteen years as an outreach counselor for Foothill College in Los Altos Hills, California before retiring and becoming a grandma. After witnessing the birth of her first grandchild, she went completely gaga! When she came back down to earth and started talking to other grandmas, she discovered they were just as crazy for their grandkids. She also realized that being a grandma was more complicated than she imagined. She had many questions about her new role and wondered what other grandmas were experiencing.

Donne enjoys creating communities of like-minded people, and so decided to start an organization for grandmas who were crazy for their grandchildren, called the GaGa Sisterhood®. In 2003 she invited all the grandmas she knew to her house to begin a conversation about what it means to be a grandma today. Over the past six years the GaGa Sisterhood has grown and now has a national following.

Donne writes a blog, an online newsletter called the GaGazine, and a monthly newspaper column called "The Go-To Grandma" for Parenting on the Peninsula. Donne and her husband live in Menlo Park, California. They have two grown children and two granddaughters. You can visit her blog at: www.gagasisterhood.com

ARLENE USLANDER

Arlene Uslander is the author of fourteen non-fiction books. She is an award-winning journalist, an essayist, and professional free-lance editor. She has had more than 400 articles published in newspapers and magazines. A retired elementary school teacher, Uslander resides in Sonora, California. Her most recent books are *That's What Grandparents Are For,* which celebrates, in illustrated verse, the very special bond between grandparents and grandchildren, and *The Simple Touch of Fate,* an anthology she co-edited, with Arizonian, Brenda Warneka, which includes over fifty fascinating stories, from people all over the world, about the role Fate plays in all our lives.

Arlene loves living so close to three of her four grandchildren, and is now trying to figure out how to get the fourth one, Ryan, who still lives in Chicago, to convince his parents that they should move to Sonora, California, too. However, Ryan is almost ready for college. A very strong bond was formed between Ryan and his grandfather ("Papa") and Arlene a long time ago, and will always remain strong.

TIM STEWART

Tim Stewart served in the Army as a military policeman. married April and raised their three children, Dawn, Shawn and Brandon in Johnsburg, Illinois. Tim retired in 1998 from the Army Reserve and Illinois Army National Guard as a Captain. In March of 2007, Tim started **Reach for Your Dreams**, to bring the leadership message to children of all ages, including corporate America, direct marketing organizations, athletic teams from junior high to the pro ranks, and schools from junior high to colleges and universities. His novel, *Positive Force* (ISBN 9781933449579 $15.95) began while Tim was convalescing from cluster headaches. He combined all of his background and experience into a story designed to reach young men and women to make a difference in their lives. The underlying message of this story is leadership. Leadership is the positive force that will not only change your life, but will change the lives of all those who know you.

Visit www.reachforyourdreams.com for more information.

CHUCK McCANN

Chuck is the first born son of a sixteen-year-old high school drop out. For most of his first seven years relatives took care of him, the next eight years Catholic Charities sheltered, fed, clothed and guided him. He dropped out of school and started working one month after he turned sixteen.

Married at twenty-one, with a child on the way, he decided to return to school, but there was a hitch. He worked as a clerk on the railroad during the evening hours, so night school was out. Instead, he attended school during the day as a regular student. It took from 1951 until 1964 to get a Master's Degree. Incidentally, he has taken a class in something every year since 1951.

He became a teacher, then a naturalist and back to teaching junior high science until he retired early due to Parkinson's Disease, which effected his ability to read and write notes on students' papers. He has taught at every level from Pre-school to college. Chuck has published four titles with Nightengale Press: three humor-filled collecitons of *Short, Shorter and Shorter Stories, Volumes I, II and III*, and *Osmis, the Cursed Egyptian Maiden*, an historical novel. Go to www.nightengalepress.com, the Our Authors Menu, for more.

SHARON BRAY

Sharon Bray is the author of two recent books, *A Healing Journey: Writing Together through Breast Cancer (2004)* and *When Words Heal: Writing through Cancer (2006)* which explore the healing benefits of writing. She has also co-edited an anthology of cancer patients' writing, *Learning to Live Again,* written and published a children's book, poetry and personal essays, one of which appeared in the anthology *Stories of Our Mothers and Fathers in Retrospect.* She is currently completing a novel. A faculty member of the UCLA extension Writer's program, Sharon lives in San Diego with her husband, John, and a neurotic toy poodle, Kramer. Her first grandchild was born February 6, 2009.

Visit her websites: www.wellspringwriters.org and www.writingthroughcancer.com for more information.

MARY PANSINI LA HAYE

Mary Pansini La Haye published her first children's book after finishing memoirs about her family. Mary, born in Los Angeles, grew up on the small ranch her dad called "San Antonio Rancho," in Montebello, California. She is a graduate of historical Ramona Convent Secondary School in Alhambra and Mount Saint Mary's College, Brentwood Heights. She majored in English and Drama. While at Mt. St. Mary's she won an Atlantic Monthly Top Paper Award. She received her Master of Arts degree at the University of Southern California, and attended summer sessions at Fordham University, New York. Her future husband, Judson A. La Haye, taught in the theater and radio department. She is now widowed, the mother of three and grandmother of nine.

Mary's books include: *It Started with a Nickel*, *Letters from Samoa*, and *A Wizard Sleeping on a Watermelon*, an ABC book for her grandchildren and everyone else's too. Mary co-authored, *The Catholic Church on Balboa Peninsula—The Story of Our Lady of Mount Carmel Parish*, a history book published in 2002.

VICTORIA ZACKHEIM

Victoria Zackheim's anthology, **THE OTHER WOMAN** (Warner Books), was released in June 2007 and went into its second printing the following week. She has appeared on **The Today Show** and **View From the Bay** (San Francisco/ABC), where she was joined by Jane Smiley, one of her anthology's authors. A reviewer in **O Magazine** was taken by the "wickedly brash survival strategy" and said it was an "unusually frank and furious collection of essays." **Associated Press** reviewer Hillary Rhodes raved that "The authors reveal a rich collection of personal sagas" and **Publishers Weekly** declared that "The main attraction of this strong collection of twenty-one personal essays is the top-drawer writers... it is a candid and truly fascinating look at how men and women love and hurt." The anthology was given a full page in **People Magazine.** Victoria has been interviewed on several radio programs and the response was excellent. Victoria is also the editor of *For Keeps: Women Tell the Truth About Their Bodies, Growing Older, and Acceptance* and *The Face in the Mirror: Writers Reflect on Their Dreams of Youth and the Reality of Age.* She teaches in the UCLA Extension Writer's Program. The author can be reached at www.victoriazackheim.com

HAL ALPIAR

A baby boomer daughter's father and grandfather of three, Hal Alpiar is founder and creative director of www.TheWriterWorks.com, Millsboro, DE, and hosts his own daily blog www.halalpiar.com for business owners/managers and entrepreneurs. A former "Professor-of-the-Year" (of business, of human development, and of creative writing), he is the author of DOCTOR BUSINESS, an Amazon 5-star selection for physicians, and DOCTOR SHOPPING, winner of a national book award for consumer health information. His poetry and feature stories (on architecture, theatre, business, healthcare, music, education, personal and professional growth and development) have been widely-published in local, regional and national magazines. He currently seeks literary agent representation for his children's self-esteem series in verse, and his newly-completed first novel HIGH TIDE.

GENE MATTHEWS

Gene grew up in rural Iowa where he spent his teenage years working on local farms. He graduated from Iowa State College (now University) in 1952 with a degree in Rural Sociology. Then he went to South Korea as a short term missionary of the Methodist Church. During those three years, he assisted in relief work and taught English while living and working on a large ecumenical agricultural project, and he married Insook Moon. Gene and Insook returned to the US and Gene enrolled in Garrett Theological Seminary, Northwestern University where he graduated with a Master of Sacred Theology degree in 1962.

Their oldest child, Mark, was born and they returned to Korea as Methodist missionaries. He attended Yonsei University's Korean Language Institute in Seoul from 1962 – 1964 and their second child, Paul, was born. Gene and Insook served in various parts of South Korea from 1964 through1997. They adopted Maria while living in Pusan. Gene's wrote numerous columns for The Korea Times, an English language daily in Seoul. He co-authored MORE THAN WITNESSES (Nightengale Press 2008). Now retired Gene is writing a book with the working title: "Humility and How I Achieved It."

VALERIE CONNELLY

Valerie Connelly divides her time between publishing, writing, composing, painting and traveling. An educator and international traveler since her days as a Peace Corps volunteer in Togo, West Africa in 1969, Valerie Connelly taught high school and college French language and literature, and English as a Second Language in Illinois from 1974-2005. She founded Nightengale Press (www.nightengalepress.com and www.nightengalepublishing.com) in July of 2003. By the end of 2009 Nightengale Press will have published more than eighty books. She has written four titles: *Sacred Night (2003)*, and *Sidetracks (2004)* both mystery-thrillers, *Arthur, the Christmas Elf (2006)* and *Calling All Authors, How to Publish with Your Eyes Wide Open (2007)*.

Valerie hosts an internet radio talk show, *CALLING ALL AUTHORS*. Listen to the extensive show archives at www.globaltalkradio.com/shows/callingallauthors where she interviews authors from all over the world and industry experts in printing, marketing, writing and publishing. Also, Ms. Connelly's paintings can be seen at www.valerieconnelly.com. Her works are available as original paintings and as prints in the ART store at www.nightengalepress.com .

REVIEWS AND GOOD NEWS

The *ART* of Grandparenting:
Loving, Spoiling, Teaching and Playing with Your Grandkids

What makes grandparents so special? Is it the unquestionable love they have for their grandchildren? Perhaps it's the freedom to spoil the little ones or spend hours telling stories. Undoubtedly, the unique bond grandparents share with their grandchildren is something that is cherished by all involved. *The Art of Grandparenting* explores the elements of this distinctive relationship in a touching and heartfelt manner.

The Art of Grandparenting is a collection of twnety essays, each written to beautifully illustrate some aspect of the child/grandparent bond. Following each article is a brief "Tips & Tricks" page which succinctly summarizes the important points in the preceding text. There is also an "About the Authors" section at the end which includes a photo and brief bio of all the contributors.

The topics covered in *The Art of Grandparenting* include a broad spectrum of concerns; all are well written and enjoyable to read. Some of these compositions are silly, witty, and humorous while others take a more serious tone. With advice from how best to get kids excited about grandpa's storytelling, to maintaining traditions, and even dealing with reluctant step-grandchildren, this book has much to offer both the new grandparent and those who are already experienced grandparents.

Rose Padrick opens the book with her essay entitled, "Open Letter to New Grandparents." Reading this article, the reader gets the sense that Rose is truly one funny lady. With lines such as "Babies smile and coo right up to the moment they are being shown off, at which time they begin a three-hour, non-stop scream fest," will keep the reader laughing throughout. Other sections will move a person to tears as he/she nods in agreement. Such is the case with Barbara Abercrombie's "Knocked Sideways By Love," where she admits that,

"...I fell in love. I didn't know how momentous – as in earth standing still, oceans roaring, heart soaring – it would feel to hold my own granddaughter..."

A refreshing aspect of this collection is that these essays don't just glamorize grandparenting with fluffy chat about how nice it is to have grandchildren. They offer specific, helpful advice on dealing with various aspects of the role of grandparent. Particularly touching was Rochelle Jewel Sharpiro's heartfelt essay, "To Grandparents-In Waiting." What happens when your grandchild, for whatever reason, simply doesn't want to be near you but only near your spouse? Rochelle was faced with this reality after her granddaughter began to associate her with the unpleasant task of enforcer. The author beautifully captures the pain she felt when rebuked but also of her intense love for her grandchild. How she resolved the problem will have readers cheering her actions and love.

Quill says: "Grandchildren are indeed your second chance to enjoy the perfection of each rose – this time without the thorns," and this book will guide you on that adventure.

Reviewed by Ellen Feld
July 2009
FEATHERED QUILL
www.featheredquill.com

The *ART* of Grandparenting: Loving, Spoiling, Teaching and Playing with Your Grandkids

"The ART of Grandparenting" is a wonderful collection of stories, humor and wisdom from several authors. Whether you are a soon-to-be, current, or seasoned grandparent, the authors' real life stories and experiences give you great insight into some good and not-so-good adventures.

This was such an easy-to-read and fun book that I look forward to using it as a gift to my friends who will be grandparents. No one tells us how to be parents, much less grandparents. We often think it is an easy job, but we find that we must conform to the parent(s) guidelines, share our grandchildren and learn through each adventure.

One of the things I particularly loved about this book is that it was not telling you what to do, but sharing experiences others have had and how they overcame any obstacles they encountered. After each story, there was a wonderful Tips and Tricks page which summarized what one had just read.

I also found it interesting, although we all want to jump in with both feet and spoil our grandchildren and help the parents, we must sometimes "watch from the sidelines without trying to coax" or intervene. I know, just like many of these authors stated, we just want to "be in the moment" and let schedules and rules fly out the window. In my own experience I have found that sometimes that is okay, but on a consistent basis it causes problems on the home front. Heaven knows I have had this "battle" with my daughter many times.

Even though we are ready to help whenever we can, we must learn that there are two sets of grandparents and we must share. This part of the book made me laugh as I'm not too good at sharing my granddaughter, even at my mature age. I really enjoyed the encouragement grandparents are given to share stories of their lives. The authors give many great suggestions on how to do this from verbal to journals to recordings.

The authors relate that there will be many times that you will not live near your grandchildren and it is important to keep in touch with them through mail, phone calls, cards or email. Also the authors suggested that we must be "flexible" in our holiday schedules. Usually during this time there are many family members to visit, and sometimes we just might have to have our holidays and visits not on the actual day.

This is such an excellent resource full of humor and is non-threatening. "The ART of Grandparenting" is a book that all should have on their shelves and read many times, especially when things get rough.

Reviewed by Carol Hoyer, PhD, for Reader Views
June 2009
www.readerviews.com

RESOURCES

OUR CONTRIBUTORS ONLINE

ARLENE USLANDER	www.uslander.net
BARBARA ABERCROMBIE	www.WritingTime.net
DONNE DAVIS	www.gagasisterhood.com
GERRI HELMS	www.lifecoadgerri.com
IRENE WATSON	www.readerviews.com
VALERIE CONNELLY	www.nightengalepress.com
HAL ALPIAR	www. halalpiar.com
TIM STEWART	www.reachforyoredreams.com
CAROLE BLAKE	www.cbpoems.com
HANNAH YAKIN	www.yakinart.com
JUDITH MAMMAY	www.judithmammay.com
ROCHELLE SHAPIRO	www.miriamthemedium.com
ROSE PADRICK	www. rosepadrick.com
SHARON BRAY	www.wellspringwriters.org
VICTORIA ZACKHEIM	www.victoriazackheim.com
CHUCK McCANN	www.npauthors.com
MARY PANSINI LA HAYE	www.npauthors.com
BOB KASCHT	www.npauthors.com

GRANDPARENTING WEBSITES

www.theartofgrandparenting.com

www.grandparents.com

www.grandmagazine.com

www.raisingyourgrandchildren.com

www.grandparentsmagazine.net

www.babybeddingtown.com

www.cricketmag.com

www.grandsplace.com

www.grandconnect.com

www.grandparenting.org

www.grandparents-day.com

www.grandmabetty.com

www.grandparentagain.com

www.nanascorner.com

And of course, you can simply type: *grandparent websites* into Google and find these and many, many more.

You can also refine your search by interest: *magazines and books for grandparents; crafts and games for grandparents; recipes for grandparents* or any subject that interests you and your grandchildren. Gardening, fishing, sewing, painting, pottery, stickers, coloringbooks, and more.

GREAT BOOKS FOR KIDS AND TEENS

All available online at
Amazon, Barnes & Noble, Borders
and at the author's websites.

CHILDREN'S PICTURE BOOKS & ILLUSTRATED STORYBOOKS

That's What Grandparents Are For
Arlene Uslander

A Wizard Sleeping on a Watermelon
Mary Pansini La Haye

The Adventures of Seamus the Sheltie   2008 ADDING WISDOM AWARD
More Tales of Seamus the Sheltie   2009 LIFE BUZZ AWARD WINNING TITLES
James Beverly
www.seamusthesheltie.com

The Punctuation Pals Meet at School
The Punctuation Pals Go to the Ball Park
The Punctuation Pals Go Snow Skiing   ALL 2005 ADDING WISDOM AWARD WINNING TITLES
The Punctuation Pals Go to the Moon
The Punctuation Pals Go to the Beach
Constance Olker

How a Real Locomotive Works   2008 BEACH BOOK AWARD WINNING TITLES
Trains and Real Locomotives
William Trombello

Arthur, the Christmas Elf   2006 ADDING WISDOM AWARD WINNING TITLE
Valerie Connelly
www.arthurthechristmaself.com

HUMOROUS POETRY FOR KIDS OF ALL AGES

Inside our Fridge
I'm Gonna Raise a Ruckus
I Am a Pie Rat
Peter Schulenburg

2005 Adding Wisdom Award Winning Title

TEEN FICTION

Positive Force
Tim Stewart

The Tales of Adarya
Alaina Buchwald

Boys Beauty & Betrayal
Camp Colorblind
JC Conrad-Ellis

TEEN NON-FICTION

Challenges — A Trip to Remember
The World Is Our Home
David Rigby

www.ingramcontent.com/pod-product-compliance
Lightning Source LLC
Chambersburg PA
CBHW061258110426
42742CB00012BA/1965